Xing Yi (Hsing I) Kung Fu for Success:
The Philosophy of Internal Power and Personal
Achievement

Xing Yi (Hsing I) Kung Fu for Success: The Philosophy of Internal Power and Personal Achievement

Lin-Cher Lee

RedWordTree Pte Ltd

2014

This publication is designed to provide competent and reliable information regarding the subject matter covered. It is sold with the understanding that the author and publisher are not engaged in rendering health, emotional, career, or other professional advice. As with anything else in life, please practise logic. Prior to the beginning of any exercise or physical regimentation, please consult a physician. If you are ill physically, emotionally or psychologically, please seek help in the form of a qualified healthcare professional or therapist. The author and publisher specifically disclaim any liability that is incurred from the use or application of the contents in this book.

First Printing: September 2014

ISBN 978-981-09-1796-8

RedWordTree Pte Ltd
111, North Bridge Road, #05-32, Peninsula Plaza
Singapore 179098

www.redwordtree.com

Dedication

Dedicated to the almighty and beloved Lord Ganesha, who has been there to lead me, guide me and assist me, such that my journey gets easier and clearer as I go along.

And to Guo Yunshen (Kuo Yun-Shen), the Xing Yi master from a long distant past, who has shown us – through example – that if we are determined to keep moving forward, nothing can stop us.

Contents

Acknowledgements

I would like to thank my teacher, Master Ge Chunyan (Ke Ch'un-Yan). She was the one who started me on this journey, and it is her teaching that has provided the catalyst for the bulk of the content of this book.

I would also like to thank my friend and business partner, Lui Natasha Amanda. Our frequent intellectual conversations and exchange of ideas have been the reason why this book is even possible. And where I have faltered, you have kept the faith. Appreciate that (inside joke) ☺, and let's work towards better years to come.

And to my ex-student, Aruna Devi, who introduced me to the Sri Layan Sithi Vinayagar Temple, the temple of Lord Ganesha. This one act of kindness – though unrequired of you – has been the source of my solace, comfort and happiness, and I wish for you all the blessings possible.

To the friendly priests at the Sri Layan Sithi Vinayagar Temple at 73, Keong Saik Road, Singapore 089167. The goodwill that you have extended to a clueless Chinese has meant more than anything else I can find in this world. I pray for the Lord God to increase my capacity and capabilities, such that I can be of greater service to the temple, and the community at large.

And to the almighty and beloved Lord Ganesha. For the bulk of my life, I was kept in the dark about who you are. Despite my ignorance, you have always been there to lead me, guide me and assist me, such that my journey gets easier and clearer as I go along.

Foreword

Even after knowing him as a colleague and friend for more than 6 years, Lin Cher still never fails to amaze.

The man is a genius, someone determined, passionate, kind, and he has been through more than his fair share of troubles to come out even better.

This book, that you are holding in your hands, is the result of 9 months of intense hard work, thinking and creativity. It also brings together the best systems and lessons that Lin Cher has seen.

If you are reading this foreword, then I'm sure that you'd have noticed by now that this isn't the same old book on reaching success.

Lin Cher has seen and learnt from many different schools of thought, but the biggest trigger that I have witnessed on his journey of self-improvement has been Xing Yi (Hsing I).

Writing about it, and sharing that information in this book, isn't surprising – it's important.

The qualities that all successful people have include focus, clarity and determination. These same qualities in Lin Cher have been honed through the system, spirit and practice of Xing Yi, and it was only the first tile of a domino effect of progress.

I hope that this book does the same thing for you.

Here's to all our success, and to the Xing Yi spirit,

Lui Natasha Amanda,
2 Sep 2014.

Preface

The pursuit of success has always been the one, singular preoccupation of mankind. Everyone desires success, and almost no one will let the promise of success pass should they be presented with one.

It is against this backdrop that modern-day charlatans of all kinds have emerged. These quacks promise to teach you their secret, if you are willing to part with a few thousand dollars from your bank account in exchange for the right to attend their "power-packed" seminars.

These motivational speakers – so to speak – will dispense common-sense advice which you would have received for free from your grandmother. Yet, you and I are suckers for their fantastical advertising, backed up by "real-life" testimonials from those who have gone on to "achieve millions" AFTER attending these "life-changing" workshops.

As someone who has succumbed to all kinds of glitzy marketing and gimmicks, I can attest to the post-workshop high that all of us experience after squandering away a few thousand dollars. For about a week after the "life-changing" event, you and I will feel at the top of the world. No challenge is too big, and NOTHING will bring us down.

But what happens after that?

It is the same old reality of the humdrum of daily living. We still have the same problems; we are still confronted with the same issues. With the fading away of the post-workshop high, nothing much has changed, except that we are poorer by a few thousand dollars.

And we have no more motivation to do anything about our lives, whatsoever.

If we are lucky, we become disillusioned and stop attending such seminars, workshops or "intensives". If we are unlucky, we still harbour hopes that there might just be a seminar, workshop or "intensive" out there that can help us "unleash" our potential. The latter scenario simply means that we would still be spending more money on things that don't work.

What if success just means taking massive, coordinated action in the direction of the goal we want to pursue? What if the lessons that these motivational speakers purportedly try to imbue in us can only be assimilated by taking action the RIGHT way? What can you do if you have always been plagued by this persistent state of INERTIA, where no amount of coaxing, exhortation or pep-talk would be able to propel you into a state of ACTION?

What can you DO to change your life for the better?

As a Chinese who has had the benefit of studying the methods and systems of the East and West, I can now say for sure that the remedy for INERTIA and INACTIVITY lies in the study of the ancient art of Xingyiquan (Wade-Giles: Hsing I Ch'uan), one of the three major internal martial art forms from China.

Granted, there are civilisations out there with a history as long as – if not more than – the Chinese civilisation. Each culture and tradition will have its own take about what constitutes success, and the right and efficient way of achieving it.

I have no interest in trying to prove that Xingyiquan is better or more superior to what these cultures and traditions are trying to teach.

But since the Chinese have a recorded history of over 5000 years, many theories and philosophies have been proposed about the different facets of life, and success is just one of the many aspects that have been covered. (To try to cover all the theories and philosophies as proposed by the Chinese throughout time would mean that I have to write an encyclopaedia, an endeavour that I would not try to undertake till the days of my retirement.)

What I am presenting here is JUST one method, and it is THE method that has worked for me, and countless others who have had the benefit of encountering the art. My presentation of Xingyiquan here does not invalidate the lessons from other cultures and traditions, and neither does it try to quash the findings of modern scientific – especially psychological – research.

But what I am going to do is to take away the HYPE from what is considered to be a simple quest which anyone can embark upon – SUCCESS. When we see everything as it is, and reduce all pursuits into one single denominator, success or the lack of it ALWAYS boils down to the presence or absence of effective action.

This is what Xingyiquan is all about. Always taking the singular, most direct and efficient action to achieve a predetermined goal.

This book has been written to give you a simple but comprehensive introduction to Xingyiquan. It will introduce you to the meaning of its name, its philosophy, its contemporaries, the people behind the art, their lives and finally the practice. I will – at appropriate times – distil the learning lessons from all that I will cover, so that you can always apply the gems from the art itself DIRECTLY into your life.

As crazy as this might sound, I am really not interested for you to READ this book. Instead, it is in my aspiration for you that after reading this book, you will seek out a good teacher in your neighbourhood to teach you the art and science of Xingyiquan itself.

Trust me; the little time and money that you invest into learning Xingyiquan will make you a far greater achiever than all the thousands and tens of thousands of dollars (not to mention the tens of hours) that you can sink into motivational workshops and seminars. Motivational seminars are all TALK; but Xingyiquan is all ACTION.

TALK versus ACTION. Which produces greater results? I will let you decide on that.

(Of course, you can always engage in a lot of talk before you take action, AS LONG as you take action.)

Introduction

As a Chinese Singaporean writing a book that is meant for Western readers, I need to do a brief introduction to the "peculiarities" that are the norm for the people of my ethnicity.

The first thing that I would like to highlight is the way Chinese names are structured. Unlike our friends from the Western world, the Chinese put their surname – or family name – in front. Thus, if Barack Obama were a Chinese, his name would be written as Obama Barack; and William Henry Gates III would be Gates William Henry III.

The next thing that I would like you to know is that there is no such thing as a first and middle name in the Chinese tradition. Each "word", or rather character, is a logogram with its own meaning, and more often than not, the second and third character in a Chinese name combine to form a unique meaning which the parents have chosen for the child.

For the purpose of this book, the official phonetic system for transcribing Mandarin pronunciations of Chinese characters has been adopted. Known as the Hanyu Pinyin, this romanisation of the Chinese language is the official system adopted by China, Taiwan and Singapore, and is taught around the world.

In the same way, all Chinese names in this book have been romanised the Hanyu Pinyin way. In every instance possible, the Wade-Giles system is provided as an alternative with each introduction of a new name. (The only exception that I have made in this book would be my name. To publish this book in the US, I have had to switch my surname to the last; and since my statutory name is not my Hanyu Pinyin name, I will have to be the odd one out in this book.)

Chapter 1: Qi (Ch'i) – The Prerequisite Of All Success

Since the dawn of Asian civilisation, the concept of a fundamental force of life has been taken to be unquestionable by the Orientals. Believed to be the energy that gives life *life*, this energy as a concept has been known by different names by the different peoples of the earth. The Japanese term Qi (Ch'i) as Ki, the Indians know it as Prana and the Chinese know it as Qi.

As much as it seems to be very much an Eastern invention, the concept of Qi has been – at various times – the subject of study by those *outside* of the Eastern sphere of influence. William Reich, an Austrian and a second-generation psychoanalyst after Sigmund Freud, termed this cosmic energy as orgone and proceeded with the controversial practice of building "orgone accumulators".

The Russians have a similar concept. They call it Bio-Plasmic energy. More adventurous souls have even proposed that the Holy Spirit in the Bible is nothing more than just another manifestation of this life force.

"And the Lord God formed man of the dust of the ground, and breathed into his nostrils *the breath of life*; and man became a living soul." Genesis 2:7

Whether Qi really exists is really not the purview or domain of this book. If the argument has gone on for centuries – trust me, not all ancient Chinese believe in Qi either – it can hardly be settled within the pages of this book.

If it really matters to you that Qi as a concept has to be verified by Western science, please feel free to read up on the subject through other publications. Enough has been written to prove and disprove the topic, and it is essential that if this is important to you, you should do what is right by confirming or debunking what will be taken as a basic assumption of this book, i.e. Qi exists and is important for your pursuit of success.

If you still don't believe me, ask Yoda.

Qi And Everyday Chinese Life

As a vital force, Qi is instrumental in the proper functioning of the many essential aspects of life.

The first and most important aspect of life where Qi plays an important role is the area of our health.

In Western medicine, the respiratory and circulatory systems are the chief driving forces of life. The concept is simple. When breathing stops, life stops; when the heart stops; life stops. Traditional Chinese Medicine (TCM) does not disagree with that. Instead, it goes one step further by adding Qi to the function. As the vital force of life, Qi drives the lungs to breathe and the heart to pump. When the Qi force is weak, so are life's other vital functions.

Due to its emphasis on Qi, it is not difficult to see how the bulk of TCM's remedies all strive to balance, unclog and promote the flow of Qi. Acupuncture, acupressure, and cupping are all attempts at making sure that Qi is flowing properly. Herbs function as an ingestible alternative to balancing Qi's ebb and flow, ensuring the right proportions of Yin (loosely translated as negative) energy and Yang (loosely translated as positive) energy in the body.

More will be said about Yin and Yang, since a proper understanding will help you grasp the reasons and direction of why and how this book is written.

The second and most notable aspect of life where Qi plays an important role is the area of architectural and interior design. Since the 1990s, the practice of Feng Shui (geomancy) has caught on in the West like storm, and is no longer a stranger to Western society much like how hamburgers have made their way to the lunch and dinner tables of the Orientals. Rather than just pure superstition, Feng Shui contains principles that are congruent with human psychology, and fit into human logic and ergonomics like hand in glove.

But due to the cultural background of the art, the ancient practitioners were UNABLE to explain concepts in modern scientific terms, using abstract and seemingly mythical concepts like White Tiger and Dragon Arteries. Like any other branch of knowledge, it is a product of its time and possesses qualities of its time.

Why am I bringing Feng Shui into the picture? I am only doing so because in inanimate objects such as buildings and houses, the Chinese have accorded them enough importance to create a subject of study so as to balance the Qi flowing in and through them, as well as its accumulation.

The last and most notable aspect of life where Qi plays an important role is the area of everyday language. Qi metaphors abound for anything and everything. For example, if something has run its course and come to the end of its lifespan, the Chinese say that it is 气数已尽 (the Qi and the days have been exhausted). If you are angry, you 生气 (Qi is rising). When you die, you 断气 (Qi has been terminated).

In short, Qi pervades every aspect of Chinese culture, and is deemed to be significant enough for humans to study its characteristics so as to manage its flow and accumulation.

Why Qi Matters

You might be wondering why I have gone to that extent of elaborating Qi and its role in everyday Chinese life. The reason is simple. If you replace Qi with the word 'vitality', you will understand why Qi is a critical element in your pursuit of success.

Using the examples given in the previous section, you will understand that:

- Your body has vitality. If you are low in vitality, you suffer ill health;
- Your home has vitality. If your home is low in vitality, you are living in a home with a 'Sick Building Syndrome';
- Everything you do has vitality. When an activity's vitality is depleted, it will come to an ominous end.

Correspondingly, to succeed in anything that you do, you need copious amounts of Qi, but you will also need to be able to manage its flow so that you don't get overwhelmed by it.

If you have observed successful people, you will see how they are always brimming with energy and always on the go. Where did they get their energy from?

Conversely, have you seen people who are always low on energy and always having this dark cloud over them? Are they successful? Are they happy? My guess is, they aren't and they probably have more problems than you and I can imagine.

How is it that the successful ones have so much vitality in them? Why is it that less successful people are always lethargic, inactive and possibly prone to inertia?

We might never get to find the answer. It might be karma, it might be a past life or it might simply be a case of upbringing. Adults who grew up in abusive environments *tend* to have less zest for life, and are *more* likely to have accumulated destructive energies in their bodily and mental systems.

NB: Please notice the italicised words. I said "tend to" and "are more likely to". I didn't say "you have to". Please do not misquote me.

But trust me. The cause is not important. I am not in the business of putting you on a couch and relating to the therapist about that favourite cat of yours that died from over-eating. I, for that matter, have had guppies that were flushed down the toilet bowl because of my angry mother. Did the occasion traumatise me? Yes, of course, it did. Did it affect my adult life? Yes, it did, but in ways that I did not expect. Was the event important? Of course it was, but you can possibly see how if we are to go through event by event everything that has happened to you that has caused issues to you, we will probably spend our whole lives talking about the past instead of living in the present.

So instead of spending too much time on the therapist's couch, why not just heal our Qi and deconstruct the bad Qi surrounding multiple, traumatic events that have occurred through the course of our lives? Events have energy, and depressing events have bad (notice how I am not using the word 'negative' here) energy.

The great thing is, Xingyiquan has the ability to help you expel this bad, toxic energy if you will allow it. The key thing is to start the practice, and allow the body to handle the rest.

Success begins when you reclaim and build your vitality. If you have always had problems starting, if you have always had problems seeing something from the beginning to the end, if you have always lacked a passion and zeal for life, and if you have always wanted to be greater than what you are right now, Xingyiquan is for you.

Disclaimer: As with all book authors, I have to put the standard disclaimer here. The content in this book is for reference and educational purposes only. It is not intended to replace professional psychiatric, psychological and medical advice. Readers with a specific need should consult a qualified healthcare professional in the relevant fields to get their symptoms treated.

It will help you accumulate more Qi in your system. It will provide the driving force for you to achieve your goals. And it will be the reason why you will ground yourself in daily activities that will propel you to achieve what you want.

Chapter 2: Developing Internally – The Way To Build Qi (Ch'i)

If vitality is essential for success, and Qi (Ch'i) is vitality, it naturally goes to say that the path to success is nothing more than just building your reserves of Qi internally, and then transmutating your reserves of vitality into tangible actions that will produce results. To do so efficiently and effectively, you need a system to develop internally, a set of methods to train, strengthen, accumulate and channel the subtle energies within you such that you can direct them outwards in a safe and productive manner.

Ultimately, I will end off by saying that Xingyiquan (Hsing I Ch'uan) is the best method out there. This book has been written with the sole aim of introducing you to this wonderful art, and I am making no excuses as to the direction of my story. But in all fairness, please do allow me to introduce you to the other art forms that might be of interest to you.

Systems To Develop Internally

There are many ways to build and accumulate Qi in your body, and one of the best ways is the practice of internal martial arts. Unlike external martial arts that place their main emphasis on brute strength, speed and physical power, internal martial arts are all about timing, precision, focus and ultimately, the cultivation of Qi.

Examples of external martial arts would include systems such as Boxing, Muay Thai, Karate, Judo, Tae Kwan Do and the Chinese Hongquan (Hung Ch'uan). Internal martial arts, on the other hand, would include examples such as Aikido, Taijiquan (T'ai Chi Ch'uan), Baguazhang (Pa Kua Chang) and Xingyiquan.

Many things can be said about the differences between external and internal martial arts, but one key difference between the two is that with the former, you tend to decline with age and with the latter, you CAN actually get better with age. There is only that much muscle and brawn that you can build, but at a certain age, you must get

PHYSICALLY weaker. The story of the older boxer defeating the much younger opponent – that's usually the stuff of Hollywood trying to comfort you that you are NOT old and that there's still hope, at least on screen.

With internal martial arts, however, the situation can be very different. At the very base level, internal martial arts are exercises that are gentle enough for those more advanced in age. Because they are usually gentler than external martial arts and most other Western-based exercises, they are easier on your joints, and you are more likely to get better and stronger with time.

In addition, their over-arching emphasis on timing, precision, focus and Qi means that your ability to fight is less dependent on how overtly fast you are, and how much force you can deliver in one punch or kick. Think Aikido and you will know what I mean.

Of course, it takes more to be a combat fighter than to just learn a few steps or moves from a martial arts form. The best fighters in Mixed Martial Arts (MMA) competitions such as the Ultimate Fighting Championships (UFC) are not just masters of combat arts, they are also able to take strong blows from the opponent before executing the final knock-out.

My role here in this book is not to convince you that Xingyiquan or the rest of the internal martial arts forms are more superior in taking down an opponent in the octagon (MMA fighting rings). There are specific rules of scoring and what is permissible and prohibited that make internal martial arts to be ineffectual as a system that can be displayed in the octagon. Even in China, the best KNOWN fighters are those who have learnt Sanshou (San Shou) – China's own version of MMA – and is an eclectic distillation of the best techniques from the various forms of Chinese kung fu.

I hope that one day, qualified fighters from the internal martial arts circles would be able to prove the efficacy of their art forms in the ring. Till then, I will be content with showing how Xingyiquan can be a good catalyst for your journey to success.

Why Xingyiquan Is The Best Internal Catalyst In Your Pursuit Of Success

Given that even in just China alone, there are already three major forms of internal martial arts, what makes Xingyiquan the greatest and the best in making you formidable in your pursuit of your own destiny?

I might be biased in my assessment, but here are my reasons.

The most popular of Chinese internal martial arts has to be Taijiquan. Comprising slow, deliberate movements that put the practitioner in a reflective, meditative state, Taijiquan has gained renown as the quintessential exercise for senior citizens. Shunned by youngsters due to its association with the old and "expired", Taijiquan has been inaccurately portrayed as either Chinese Yoga or super-low impact aerobics.

As with any kind of popular perception related to any topic of any kind, the public's understanding of Taijiquan is filled with half-truths and loads of misinformation. An art that was once the sole prerogative of the inhabitants of the Chen Village in Henan Province, Yang Luchan (Yang Lu-Ch'an) became the first non-Chen to master the art and introduced it to the rest of China in Beijing.

The original Chen Style of Taijiquan is more dynamic, explosive and combative than the gentler, slower Yang Style you witness in public parks today. Because it is really so much more sophisticated than it looks, students who really master the art are rare and few. The most that *ordinary* students can manage is to expertly execute it as an exercise.

Why and how such a dynamic art became an old man's form is too long a story to cover in this book.

Because all Chinese martial arts are philosophies in action, you will need to understand that Taijiquan is all about overcoming hard, brute force with soft power – which also explains its circular movements that are more deflective than confrontational.

Baguazhang, though about two hundred years of age, is a relative newcomer in the public stratosphere. Created by Dong Haichuan (Tung Hai-Ch'uan) during the latter part of the Qing (Ch'ing) dynasty, the art has enjoyed new limelight due to Zhang Ziyi's (Chang Tzu-I) portrayal in Wong Kar-Wai's epic movie, The Grandmaster. Like Taijiquan, Baguazhang is characterised by circular movements, but these movements are wider and have a longer reach than Taijiquan. Like what you will see in Zhang Ziyi's acting, Baguazhang exponents walk around an imaginary Trigram or Bagua while twisting and turning around a hypothetical opponent.

At its very core, Baguazhang's main philosophy is to be the constant in the fluctuating world of variables. Despite the multiple twists and turns, the practitioner stays true to the centre line, which runs from the top of the head through the spine and to the ground.

While Taijiquan and Baguazhang both have lessons and philosophies that hold relevance to the world today, the depth of study required to apply them becomes a hindrance – if not a put-off – in the fast-moving societies we live in today. Since Y2K, the assumptions we hold true can no longer be left unquestioned. Once infallible institutions such as the Lehman Brothers have since vanished into obscurity. Internet technologies have migrated from the desktop to the smartphones, and the level of connectivity we enjoy today is beyond what could be imagined a decade ago.

In the global arena, the balance of power is threatening to shift and the world is disturbed. Within less than ten years, China has risen from obscurity to a global commercial powerhouse. Its increasing confidence also means that it is now asserting its presence in a way that it has never done before, causing unease among its neighbours and traditional superpowers such as the United States.

Youths in Europe, used to the good life, find themselves at the short end of the employment spectrum. People are disgruntled and disillusioned. In short, the world has become more uncertain, definitely messier and more disorderly to say the least.

To master the new world – where uncertainties run high – it is essential that we are clear in our mind and bold in our actions. As an ancient adage says,

---

Fortune favours the bold.

We need to be brave and decisive. We need to charge towards our goals without doubt and fear. Our actions and intentions must match. Our mind and body must move together as one.

In a world that changes at the speed of thought, we need to adopt a mindset and attitude that know no fear. Those who know Xingyiquan's history term it the "Guo Yunshen (Kuo Yun-Shen) attitude". I will introduce who Guo Yunshen is and what this crazy guy did during the course of his lifetime, but the study of Xingyiquan can imbibe in you the mindset and attitude that will help you thrive in such turbulent times.

In case you think that Taijiquan and Baguazhang are not worth the study, please allow me to make my stand clear. All three Chinese internal martial arts have a history dating back at least two hundred years, and are the distillation of the best of Chinese philosophies into sequences of movements that allow you to NOT just master martial arts, but also INTERNALISE the principles, legacies and power behind them. On its own, Xingyiquan is inadequate as a philosophy of life. You will become too direct, no-nonsense and somewhat too aggressive for anyone's liking. And that's where Taijiquan and Baguazhang come in to mitigate the effects.

If it is success that you want to pursue, Xingyiquan is the fastest and most direct way to build internal power such that you become focused on that one goal you want to attain. The secret lies in its principles, characteristics and movements, all of which were designed to transform you into a relentless go-getter unstoppable in your path.

"Are you telling me that if I learn Xingyiquan, I will automatically become a motivated and relentless go-getter?"

Yes, and to cover my own arse a bit, I would say, *ceteris paribus*, Xingyiquan will transform you into an unyielding achiever.

You will discover within yourself this strength, this resolve to always go on despite the disappointments that you will face. You will realise that even if you trip, you will bounce back up every time to face your opponent, your stumbling block, your difficulties squarely and bravely.

Am I promising too much? Maybe, but I want you to start learning the art instead of rationalising, thinking and debating what I am saying. Too much talk and no action basically gets us nowhere; and no other time has there been a situation where we are plagued by simply too much talk.

Chapter 3: Embrace The Path, The Power, The Philosophy

Because there is YouTube today, it wouldn't be difficult for you to find a video of Xingyiquan (Hsing I Ch'uan) online. And if you watch the video, you will realise something: Xingyiquan is too fast, too dynamic to be a form of internal martial arts. The conventional impression of internal martial arts is that of slow, gentle movements à la Taijiquan (T'ai Chi Ch'uan) and Baguazhang (Pa Kua Chang). Then how is it that such a strong, formidable art is classified alongside its softer, more circular cousins?

To understand this, we would have to delve into the deep, profound and perhaps illustrious history of Xingyiquan, and we can begin our appreciation of this wonderful art by first knowing the meaning of its name.

To be completely biased, I believe there is no other form of martial art or branch of knowledge that is as unified, coordinated and synchronised from the very beginning to the end.

The 'Xing' (形) in Xingyiquan (形意拳) means form, shape, structure or pattern; and the character is used to denote the external manifestation of the art. This manifestation is reflected in the stance, techniques, methods and sequences taught to students of Xingyiquan.

The 'Yi' (意) in Xingyiquan, on the other hand, means intention, will, purpose or deliberation; and the character is used to denote the internal components that precede the external manifestation of the art. In the 'Yi' portion of Xingyiquan, it is always about what YOU want to achieve. Are you out to bring down your opponent? Or are you just out to distract a potential attacker such that you can find a means to escape?

Whatever you adopt as 'Xing' in terms of the moves you execute is ABSOLUTELY dependent on what you WANT as part of your 'Yi'; therefore the name 'Xingyi'.

The 'Quan' (拳) in Xingyiquan has traditionally been translated as 'Boxing' in most Western literature. Although the word literally means 'fist', it actually refers to a system or way of fighting, much like the word '*do*' in 'Judo', 'Karate Do' or 'Tae Kwan Do'. To cut it short, the word 'Quan' can be taken as synonymous to 'Do', but because the Chinese are too grounded in hard realities, they (we) prefer to call it a system of fighting rather than use an abstract term such as "*the way*".

At its very core, Xingyiquan is a form of martial arts that places undue emphasis on the coordination between mind and body; synchronisation of goal and methods; and the unification of plan and action. It is a study that trains the student to go for what he wants in the most direct, unabashed way.

And because of this, Xingyiquan moves are mostly linear, since the shortest distance between any two objects would be a straight line. (Of course, if you are into Quantum Physics, your definition of what constitutes the shortest distance between two objects would differ.)

The importance that Xingyi (from this moment onwards, we will use the terms 'Xingyiquan' and 'Xingyi' interchangeably) places on driving through with full force into attacking your opponent simply means that the moves will neither be fanciful nor beautiful. In some ways, they look ugly vis-à-vis other known but more spectacular martial arts.

If you are out to impress with your martial arts skills, Xingyiquan will make a poor choice as a martial art to learn and demonstrate. Showing off your Xingyi moves to a gaggle of chicks you want to impress is not just poor judgement, it is plain stupid. You will screw your date chances, and the chicks that you are trying to date will think that you are a cock. (But chicks and cocks make a good combo.)

If, however, you are looking for something simple to learn and easy to apply, Xingyiquan will make a good – if not the best – candidate of choice.

Why Learn Xingyiquan

At this point of the book, you might be wondering why you should learn Xingyiquan since even the author of the book – which is me – has expressed doubt about the effectiveness of this form of martial art in a bout in the octagon. And since you aren't going to do well impressing the chicks with this art, you might as well not even bother considering it, since it would seem *useless* to learn a form of combat that is two hundred years old?

The answer lies in what Xingyiquan can do for you *other* than combat.

As a martial art that focuses on coordinating and synchronising your moves with your intention, it has incorporated – within its training – elaborate principles that will ensure that your mind, body and soul move together as one. For example, in Xingyiquan training, there is the concept of the Three Points of Coordination, both externally and internally.

Externally, the hands should coordinate with the feet, the elbows should coordinate with the knees and the shoulders should coordinate with the hips.

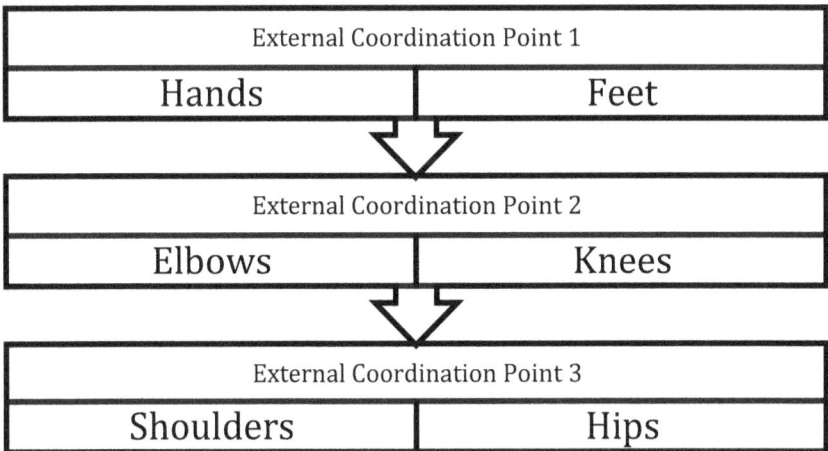

External Coordination Point 1	
Hands	Feet

External Coordination Point 2	
Elbows	Knees

External Coordination Point 3	
Shoulders	Hips

Internally, the mind should coordinate with the intention, the intention should coordinate with the Qi while the Qi should coordinate with the power.

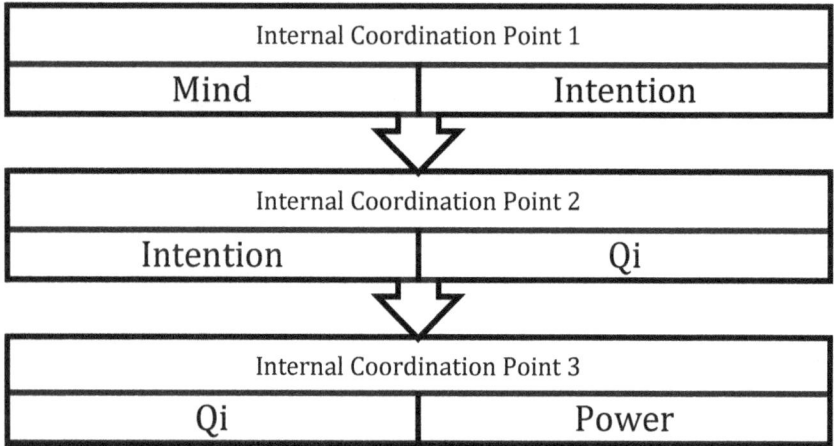

Internal Coordination Point 1	
Mind	Intention

Internal Coordination Point 2	
Intention	Qi

Internal Coordination Point 3	
Qi	Power

Because Xingyiquan is essentially a massive exercise in coordination between what you want and feel *inside*, and the kind of action and movements that you will undertake *outside*, the art itself is the best of experiential learning that you can find, with concrete experience that will serve as a base that you can reflect upon and derive lessons from.

You might be surprised how this simple concept of always undertaking actions in line with your objectives to be sorely lacking in people.

For example, if you bitch about your boy or girlfriend to your friends, don't be too offended if your concerned friends tell you to leave him or her. Because your friends are concerned about you, it would be hard for them to relate that you are just bitching about your partner.

In the same way, if you wanted to be a writer of English fiction, the first thing you will need is a good grasp of the written English language. If you are sorely lacking – let's say – in grammar skills, you would do well if you decided to go for grammar classes so that you could improve in your writing, instead of hoping or praying to be recognised as a good writer.

And for that matter, let's say that you have no money and you are stressed. It will be better for you to take up a part-time job or something that makes you money, rather than take up meditation since you have heard that meditation helps to reduce stress. In this scenario, the money is the issue, so going the INDIRECT route of trying to cut down on stress through meditation isn't going to work very well.

Too many a time, the solutions to our problems are simple and straightforward, but we complicate the situation by our warped thinking and crazy mental attachments.

The last thing that I want to handle in this chapter is the Law of Attraction. Since the launch of the bestseller, The Secret, there has been a lot of talk about using the MIND to draw in the subject of your affection. My business partner and I used to know of someone who believed it so much that she was truly convinced that ALL she had to do was just imagine.

She believed that as long as she BELIEVED, everything that she wanted would come to her, and she would have to do NOTHING about it.

Seriously, I haven't seen or met anyone more deluded than that.

Nothing that I have said in this chapter or the rest of the book invalidates the Law of Attraction. As a spiritual person by nature, I truly believe that your vibes can affect a lot of things around you.

But unknown to many people, the Law of Attraction, being a derivative from the original Master Key System by Charles F Haanel, requires concrete action and effort for manifestation to come true. Whatever you conceive in your MIND can only come true if you take ACTION for it to come true. In short, there is a price – or something of value – on your end to be given in EXCHANGE for what you want. The Law of Attraction only kicks in to make it easier.

And this is what Xingyi is all about. It is about knowing CLEARLY what you want, making UNAMBIGUOUS moves, and taking DECISIVE steps towards what you want. The nature of the art reflects this, where the punches and strikes are evidently out to take down the opponent.

It would be a lot easier for your friends, family and the universal forces to support you if you know exactly what you want, and if you are acting in congruence with what you want.

It is perhaps appropriate at this point in time to bring in the case of Belle Knox (her stage name, real name unknown), the Duke University freshman who starred in porn shows so as to fund her college education. At the point of writing, news of this girl has spread far and wide, and she is the target of bullying on and off campus because of her "profession".

Morals aside (and seriously, which set are we supposed to apply), I find this young lady totally deserving of respect. Despite her controversial career choice, her intention to pay for her college tuition – amounting to US$60,000 per year – on her own without putting the financial burden on her family is worthy of anyone's admiration. Plus, she was clear enough about her options. Typical student jobs definitely won't pay enough to cover US$60,000 per year (if you know of one, please let me know), and unless she puts herself in excessive liability – if the bank grants her a 100% loan, she would be saddled with a debt of US$240,000 by the end of four years – there is just no way to stay in college.

Please get this straight: I am not saying that becoming a porn actress is to be encouraged. But comparing the person we knew with Belle Knox, Belle is definitely clearer about what she wants and how to get there.

To me, that's all I need to respect her for her choice.

Her move is very Xingyi-like. And she is a much better person than the person we knew. (You can choose to disagree with that.)

Chapter 4: Guo Yunshen (Kuo Yun-Shen) – The Motivational Doer, Not Speaker

No book on Xingyiquan (Hsing I Ch'uan) would be complete without a feature on legendary Xingyi master, Guo Yunshen (Kuo Yun-Shen). Guo Yunshen (1829 – 1898) was a Xingyiquan master most well-known for his "half-step crushing punch", but if nature had been allowed to take its course, he might never have become the great fighter that he was later known to be.

You see, Guo Yunshen was a ruffian. I mean, martial artists are, in general, not very nice people, but Guo Yunshen, he was in a different league altogether. This man loved to fight, and at every available opportunity, would challenge another opponent to a duel.

Li Luoneng (Li Luo-Neng), the master whom he approached to teach him, recognised this and refused to accept him as a student. Guo Yunshen, however, would not be deterred. How he did this would continue to be a great unknown, but legend has it that Guo Yunshen was able to disguise himself as a workman so that he could gain access to Li's house. For three continuous years, the determined Guo surreptitiously observed what Li Luoneng was teaching to his students; and what he surreptitiously learned, he fervently practised.

For the three years he was masquerading as a workman, Guo Yunshen was obsessed with practising the Bengquan (Peng Ch'uan) (Crushing Punch) that he saw Li teaching his students. It was probably due to the limitations of trying to learn a martial art while trying to ensure that your cover as a workman was not blown; it is really hard to master a full set of martial arts moves when you have to do tasks assigned to you, yet you know you are not really there for the job.

Among the Five Elemental Punches, the Bengquan is the easiest to learn, and the constraints imposed on Guo wouldn't allow him to master more than the one move that he was destined to learn.

Soon, three years passed in the blink of an eye. By this time, Guo Yunshen had become a master of just one move – the Bengquan. Approaching Li Luoneng once again and revealing his identity, Guo demonstrated the one move that he could execute to Li. Seeing how Guo Yunshen was able to perfect the Bengquan without being taught, Li relented and agreed to accept Guo Yunshen as his student.

Guo's persistence and dedication had paid off.

(How Guo was able to hide his identity is a big unknown. Maybe he had access to the face transplant surgery available in Face/Off.)

The Guo Yunshen Mindset

If you haven't realised, Guo Yunshen was a man who would not take "No" for an answer. Despite Li Luoneng's earlier refusal, Guo was undeterred in his quest to learn and master Xingyiquan. It is this determination that allowed him to take the foot-in-the-door route, disguising himself as a lowly workman, and painstakingly observing, learning all he could whilst ensuring that his cover remained a cover.

When he later revealed his true identity and intentions, it was a sales pitch that could not be ignored – "I will master Xingyiquan with or without your permission, but you will make everyone happier if you agree to teach me". Faced with such a compelling proposition, it is no wonder that Li Luoneng eventually agreed to take him in; in actual fact, I think he didn't have much of a choice.

Guo Yunshen In Prison

The best predictor of future behaviour is past behaviour. If you thought that Guo Yunshen was going to change because Li Luoneng had accepted him as a student, please think again. Already, prior to Li even taking him in as a student, he had created a reputation for himself as a rough and violent person. (I simply summarised it into the word 'ruffian' in the previous section.) Li recognised this and would have none of it; unfortunately for him, Guo Yunshen was too dogged in his pursuit of Xingyiquan.

Under Li's tutelage and guidance, Guo Yunshen improved in leaps and bounds; better still, his Bengquan (Crushing Punch) was gaining fame far and wide. To Guo Yunshen, life couldn't be better. As someone who would not shy away from a fight – sorry, correction, as someone who was always looking for a fight – Guo Yunshen was having a good time, taking down opponents and defeating them with the Bengquan (Crushing Punch) he had painstakingly taken years to perfect. It was almost as if Guo was creating his own MMA championships in ancient China; ancient being about two hundred years ago.

This MMA party would come to a halt for about three years when Guo Yunshen would accidentally kill someone in a fight.

Accounts differ about what actually happened. In one story, Guo was challenged by another pugilist for a duel. As someone who would not shy away from a fight – in fact, I dare deduce that he would actually relish in one – Guo went ahead to show how he was the superior fighter; better-skilled and possessing more prowess. However, it was also this obsession with victory that would land him in trouble. Eager to once again demonstrate his formidable Bengquan (Crushing Punch), Guo was too fast and too forceful to be handled by anyone. In no time, his opponent was spitting blood, and in less time, he kicked the bucket. For this, Guo was incarcerated for three years. I guess MMA fights in ancient China ranked poor in safety standards.

The other story differed in the sense that Guo was not fighting a martial arts exponent; instead, he was taking on a local thug. You see, while Guo was a ruffian, it was more of a personality trait rather than a character flaw. Chinese martial artists – especially those of yesteryear – believe that they have a duty to rid the world of evil and to stand up for the weak. Guo Yunshen took this too seriously.

[Yes, he loved to challenge others, but it was more of a desire to confirm that he was good than to kill. One needs to remember that for such a hard fighter like him, incidents of him killing another was zilch, other than the one that we are trying to decipher here. In fact, he was known to treat those whom he had injured (martial artists had to be somewhat Chinese physicians as well), once again evidence that he was not a brute out to kill, but a practitioner out to test, prove and disprove what he had learned. He recognised that those he was sparring with were not his enemies, but "test subjects" so to speak. (This reminds me of stories of another more famous Chinese martial artist, Bruce Lee. As a young man, Bruce was eager to test out those moves he had learnt. Thus, after learning a few moves from his master, Ip Man, he would go on the streets, taunt the British boys walking by and get into a scuffle. When the techniques worked, he would win; when they didn't, he would run.)]

But with the villain, it was a different story. Feeling great injustice, Guo Yunshen gave him a piece of his mind, totally forgetting that most accomplished martial artists would have a hard time with him, much less a local villain. In short, the arsehole got killed, and Guo was sent to prison.

No matter what the cause of the homicide was, it is agreed that Guo did get imprisoned, and three years was an indisputable fact. There is something about Chinese prisons that I need to highlight here. Whether it was in the past or now, China has always had a bad record with human rights. To understand the scale of this abuse, one needs to know what the ultimate punishment in China was. In ancient China, the worst punishment you can get is extermination to nine levels of kinship (株连九族). Usually reserved for serious crimes against the state such as treason – which basically means the "criminal" did something that stepped on the toes of the Emperor (like bedding his women, which numbered more than 3,000) – this extermination would extend to everyone within the criminal's own and extended family. These poor souls to be beheaded would include:

- The criminal's living parents;
- The criminal's living grandparents;
- The criminal's children (if any);
- The criminal's grandchildren (if any);
- The criminal's siblings and siblings-in-law;
- The criminal's uncles, as well as their spouses; and, of course
- The criminal himself.

You can see how inhumane this system was. The extent of abuse is beyond what a Western mind can imagine. And it was a fact that every Chinese living under the skies of China had to contend with. You would have to pray, hope, wish, and beg that everyone within your immediate and extended family is a law-abiding citizen. You would have to hope that your irritating in-laws are not revolutionaries fighting to overthrow the current Emperor and dynasty. And you would really hope that none of your grown siblings or their husbands and wives would step on the wrong toes in the Imperial Court. 草煎人命, the blatant inflicting of suffering or killing of another human, was (I hope it is not 'is') a rampant phenomenon in China.

{On another note, the Chinese judicial system had been – I mean, has been – well-known for all sorts of miscarriages of justice. Assuming the accused to be guilty before proven innocent, the judge or magistrate presiding a case would have no qualms using torture as a means to extract a confession. There was no such thing as access to a lawyer, and more often than not, those wrongly accused would confess so that they did not have to suffer pain. [If there was anything *good* that came out of this, the Manchu government during the Qing (Ch'ing) dynasty created a system of torture, aptly termed "The Ten Major Ways of Torture during the Qing Dynasty". What goes around comes around. In a strange twist of fate, the Chinese commoner would indirectly suffer at the hands of their government years later when the Japanese employed the same modes of torture during the Second Sino-Japanese War.]}

If a common man in the good old days of China had so much that could *potentially* go against him where justice was concerned, one could imagine what prison could actually be like. A typical Chinese prison was nothing more of a dungeon; sanitation was close to non-existent and typically, they feed you like you would feed a dog (I am thinking stray dogs, not those lucky dogs featured in Cesar Millan's Dog Whisperer.) And because human rights abuse was the rule of the day, one can easily imagine how a prisoner would be treated.

Due to how hard, inhumane and *shitty* (pardon the pun) prison life could get, most inmates would take their jail term as a death sentence. Against this backdrop of disease, starvation, infection and potential abuse, most ordinary people would have given up the will to live, since death would look like the ultimate eventual outcome that would materialise.

But what did Guo Yunshen do? He continued practising his Xingyiquan.

But there were constraints. Classified as "dangerous" and befitting of the highest security prison available, Guo's hands were manacled while his legs were chained together by shackles.

Because his movements were restricted, Guo could no longer lunge the full distance forward; his lunges were now half the distance of what it used to be. Practising his favourite Bengquan (Crushing Punch), Guo Yunshen would soon perfect the one move that he would be known for, usually translated as "Half Step Crushing Punch" but more accurately translated as "Half Lunge Crushing Punch" (Chinese to English translation is really difficult).

Three years would come and go, and Guo Yunshen was soon released.

Remember the guy he killed? Well, whoever it was, his followers or disciples decided that it was payback time for the death of their leader or master. Thinking that Guo would have deteriorated in strength, speed and power due to malnutrition, ill health and possibly depression, these monkeys saw it fit to take on Guo Yunshen in his supposedly "weakened" state.

Unfortunately for them, they were wrong in their assessment. Due to his Prison Bengquan Boot Camp, Guo wasn't any weaker, but stronger. Using shackles and fetters as weights and the chains that bound them as resistance bands, Guo was in a better position to take on his MMA bouts. Although his lunge had become shorter in distance – a three-year habit is hard to change – his power and his speed had become more remarkable. In short, the *avengers* were defeated, and Guo was the winner once again. (Fortunately for the *avengers*, they lived to tell their story. Guo obviously didn't kill them since he never got incarcerated again.)

Because of this, Guo Yunshen made a name for himself using his "Half Lunge Crushing Punch". There is even a saying for this in the Xingyi circles: "半步崩拳打遍天下无敌手", which basically explains the phenomenon of Guo defeating his opponents with only his Half Lunge Crushing Punch.

Guo Yunshen And Dong Haichuan (Tung Hai-Ch'uan)

The final story about Guo Yunshen is his *supposed* battle with Dong Haichuan (Tung Hai-Ch'uan).

At this point in time, it would be appropriate to highlight the difficulties associated with researching events that happened in China a while ago, a while meaning a couple of hundred years ago. At least two hundred years ago, news reporting – as we know it today – was non-existent. The bulk of China was illiterate, with most commoners involved in farming and agriculture-related trades. Against that kind of background, it would not be hard to see how official documentation of events would be sorely lacking.

In addition, even if someone were to document the events that happened, there would be an issue as to what to focus on. By 1860, when Guo Yunshen was about thirty-one years of age, the population of China was already about 377 million. Contrast this with the approximately 28 million in the United Kingdom and the 31 million in the United States of America at that time and you would know how difficult it was (it still is) to decide what to focus on. (Even today, the population of America is 317 million, about 60 million less than the population of China in 1860.)

Because of this, many records of what happened were highly dependent on the eyewitness accounts of what the people around saw and heard. Since everyone interprets the same events differently, it would not be uncommon to hear multiple versions of the same thing. To make things worse, it is human nature to embellish these stories while relating to another interested party, making the simple story of a sparring session into an epic tale of heroism, brotherhood and respect for another.

It would be easier if they had YouTube, Instagram or something like that; life would be easier for someone like me, trying to relate their stories to you.

Given the constraints imposed upon the times then, I can only sort of talk about this *supposed* battle between Dong Haichuan and Guo Yunshen. In a previous chapter, I gave a short introduction to Baguazhang (Pa Kua Chang). Well, Dong Haichuan was the creator of this form of martial arts. Being a formidable man in his own right, it was going to be a matter of time that these two men were going to challenge each other to a duel. Whoever initiated the match would never be known.

According to the very exaggerated version of the story, Dong and Guo fought each other over three days and nights. Seriously, how do you do that? Did they take breaks? Did they have a referee? Was someone responsible for calling a time-out? Well, we'll never know.

The legend states that neither of the two was able to defeat the other. In the end, there was this mutual respect that each had for the skill level and competence of the other, so it was decided that students of the Xingyi and Bagua school would cross-train with each other.

So while the event was – once again – disputable, the outcome was the same. Since that supposed duel, students of Xingyiquan have been learning Baguazhang, and vice versa. It was a logical thing to do. Xingyiquan, being more linear and direct, would benefit from Baguazhang's spiralling, circular and waist-twisting movements, while students of Bagua can learn from Xingyi's more direct, and forthcoming ways. The tradition has lasted till today; most students learn Xingyiquan and Baguazhang together.

(A more sceptical part of me says that Guo Yunshen and Dong Haichuan came up with a superb affiliate/referral marketing programme that would benefit both schools.)

What Guo Yunshen Demonstrated To The World

Although relatively short in stature, Guo Yunshen showed how it is not just the size of your body, but how you coordinate everything into one singular fighting unit that matters. Not only that, he also showed how Xingyiquan is an extremely effective form of combat.

(As a note, the one key rule when we evaluate any form of Chinese martial arts is whether it has been able to survive the passing of time. Can an effective and efficient form of Chinese martial art be lost in time? Yes, definitely. Because in olden China, there have been patriarchs who insist on ONLY passing their art to sons and those within the family. In such cases, there is a chance the art might die out, either because the patriarch had no son, or his son was useless or uninclined towards martial combat.

But those combat systems that did not make the cut would definitely be lost. This is because of what I would term to be a "natural elimination system" that was prevalent in the olden past. In ancient times, there was this need to prove that the art you were teaching was more superior to another. Due to this, challengers coming to your school, initiating a match was common. If you lost too frequently, you would lose all your students, which also meant that your school would shut down.)

But more than showing us that he could fight, Guo also showed us the way to success in the things he did, and the response he had in the face of difficulties. Since Guo was never really a talker, I – the writer – would have to derive lessons from the things he did and compile them into a list of axioms that we can all easily follow.

1. If circumstances hold you back, always find another way.

    Most of us would have given up in the face of rejection. However, for Guo Yunshen, his clear-mindedness about what he wanted allowed him to take another route to his goal. Disguising himself as a workman was Step One; clandestinely learning the Bengquan (Crushing Punch) was Step Two; presenting himself to Li Luoneng again was Step Three.

2. Master one skill VERY well.

In a world of information overload, most of us fall into the trap of becoming jacks of all trades but masters of none. Not for Guo though. Throughout his martial arts career that lasted till he died, Bengquan was his one obsession even as he went on to master the other aspects of Xingyiquan.

3. Use every setback as impetus to advance and progress.

Most of us would wallow in self-pity, feel depressed when something bad happens to us. "Why me?" is the single question that would resonate in our heads. For Guo Yunshen, he didn't really bother. For a man who was always doing, he continued in prison what he had always been doing outside: practise.

Diligence and resilience in whatever he was doing – no matter what the circumstance – was Guo's way to success. (As a side note, I don't think that Guo was devoid of emotions. As a man of intensity, he must have felt the injustice and sadness of being imprisoned, but since there was nothing he could do about it – a homicide did occur – he might as well embrace the circumstances and make the best use of them.)

4. Actively look for bigger challenges.

Throughout his whole life, Guo was always on the quest to find opponents better than himself. His *supposed* battle with Dong Haichuan – though unproven – was in line with his character and belief. Real learning takes place when we stretch ourselves beyond our perceived ability and limits. For Guo, his way of "stretching" was to take on worthy opponents. We can definitely take a page off Guo's book and learn from his ongoing quest to become the best (though we shouldn't emulate his *somewhat* reckless fighting attitude).

5. When you meet a master, collaborate with him.

When Guo and Dong failed at taking the other down, they did the most enlightened thing that anyone can do: collaborate with each other. Since one is as good as the other despite their different systems, it is only logical that they came up with a way of collaboration that would be mutually beneficial.

The Guo Yunshen Success Principles In A Nutshell

1. If circumstances hold you back, always find another way.
2. Master one skill VERY well.
3. Use every setback as impetus to advance and progress.
4. Actively look for bigger challenges.
5. When you meet a master, collaborate with him.

Chapter 5: How To Stand Your Ground; How To Always Move Forward

Just like how the foundation of English is grammar and vocabulary, the fundamental of all Chinese martial arts is the ability to adopt a strong and powerful stance. Like the age-old adage, you must learn how to stand before you learn how to walk, and you must learn how to walk before you learn how to run (I actually have a friend who learnt how to run before she learnt how to walk). A stance is just a way for you to stand rooted to the ground, so that all your other techniques can come forth in a stronger and more explosive way.

Without solid grounding, all your other techniques would be fantabulous displays, all fluff but no real power. You won't be able to drive through with your attacks, and even if you do get to hit your opponent, the damage that you will inflict will be minimal. (All martial arts moves are made to kill, injure or maim; if they don't, you are giving a massage.)

The same requirement applies to Xingyiquan (Hsing I Ch'uan) training. As a Chinese combat art, it contains stances that are found in other forms of Chinese martial arts. As an internal martial art form, however, it proudly holds a stance that is not widely practised in the other external forms like Hongquan (Hong Ch'uan) or Shaolinquan (Shao Lin Ch'uan). This stance is called Santishi (San T'i Shih) (三体式), which looks like this:

In essence, Santishi is more of a posture rather than a stance. "San", meaning three in Mandarin, is a reflection of a pre-eminent Daoist (Taoist) philosophy of alignment between Heaven (meaning the cosmic universe), Earth (reality) and Mankind (You and I). (My explanations in the parentheses are in no way exclusive; Chinese language, on its own, suffers from the plague of ambiguity and imprecision because any one character has multiple meanings at any one time, but it is also this ambiguity that allows it the flexibility of capturing the vastness of the universe.) When misalignment happens, disaster results.

Santishi is the physical manifestation of this proposed alignment, with the head held high, holding up the heavens, and the feet firmly grounded *in*, not *on*, the earth. The practitioner is the human right in between. Weight is unevenly distributed, with the front leg only taking on 40% of the body weight, and the rear leg taking on the remaining 60%. The back is held straight, with a slight (very slight) backward-leaning tendency. The extended arm is held at the level of the chest, while the other arm is held firmly against the belly, where the navel is. Both hands will adopt an open-palm position.

As a combat stance, Santishi differs from other combat forms in that most other forms tend to place the bulk of the body weight on the front leg rather than the rear leg. Furthermore, the open palm position is adopted; other forms – whether Chinese or non-Chinese – tend to adopt the fist and not the palm.

Due to the limitations of a printed book, there is very little I can do here to show you what Santishi looks and feels like, other than the picture shown earlier. However, in the digital age, this problem can be easily solved by a YouTube search. Please feel free to go online and search for a demonstration of Santishi. **Please note one thing though**: if the demonstrator is not putting more of his body weight on his rear leg, he is NOT demonstrating correctly and knows NUTS about Xingyiquan (I am only writing this because I have seen a "Master" demonstrating Santishi and leaning his body forward. I know that there are quite a few denominations under Xingyiquan, but no matter which school you are learning from, Santishi is the same, with a backward-leaning tendency and the bulk of the body weight on the rear leg. If these "masters" don't get this basic right, I don't see how they can even be qualified to teach you Xingyiquan.)

(Another thing I need to highlight about this book. All illustrations of martial arts moves are comic portrayals only. They are NOT intended to be copied for practice. If you seriously want to learn, find a master.)

The Truth About Santishi

Most students of Xingyiquan (sadly) don't see it, but Santishi is as much a martial arts posture as it is a philosophy of life. Planting your feet firmly into the ground, and standing strongly with your head held high, are things that all of us need to do in both martial arts and life. Beginners learning Santishi will usually be told by their teachers to do this rocking motion, where you feel stepping into the ground with your front and rear feet. And mind this paradox: although you have to plant yourself into the ground, the posture should be relaxed and correct.

The extended arm keeps your enemy at a distance, so that you will be safe without having to unnecessarily fear an attack. The other palm is placed at the belly, where all power originates.

The end product of Santishi is a metaphor for life. Keep your distance, not just from your enemies, but friends and relatives. How many times in life have we been too friendly, and our supposed friends and family start imposing on us, without due regard for boundaries. We end up angry, frustrated and our relationships get soured. All this could have been avoided had we made it **clear** that our personal space – demarcated by our extended arm – has to be respected. (As I said earlier, Xingyi moves are clear and unambiguous.)

The importance of grounding in Xingyiquan was not lost on the early Xingyi masters. Guo Yunshen (Kuo Yun-Shen), the guy from the previous chapter, was the first person to formally incorporate Santishi training as an integral part of Xingyi training. In fact, Santishi was deemed to be so important that students of Xingyi were required to train in the posture for three full years before they were taught anything else.

[Of course, there's another part of me that believes that Guo was trying to extend the programme so that he could charge more training fees. And if you haven't realised, the Chinese seem to have an obsession over the number '3'. There is a saying in Chinese that states that with consistent effort, success will be evident at the three-year mark, while phenomenal success will be witnessed at the five-year mark (三年一小成，五年一大成). If Guo wasn't out to scam his students – which I don't think he was (martial arts teachers in those days were, in general, unusually demanding by today's standards) – he was definitely ensuring that his students had some success in grounding themselves properly before they moved on. Or maybe he read Malcolm Gladwell's book.]

(Of course, I still think that Guo was a psychopath.)

As the fundamental posture in Xingyiquan, it is the start point of many cool moves that you will witness later (in illustrated version) in the next few chapters of the book.

The Truth About Santishi In A Nutshell

No	Santishi Requirements	Life Lessons Based On Santishi
1	Stay grounded.	Always ground yourself in the hard realities of the situation.
2	Hold your head up high.	Be confident and stay positive.
3	Keep your back straight.	Grow a spine and have lots of courage.
4	Lean backwards slightly	Trust in your innate ability to do well.
5	Look your opponent in the eyes.	Don't shy away from your problems; tackle them head-on.
6	Extended arm should be almost completely outstretched.	Keep your distance, set clear boundaries about personal space, what is acceptable and what is unacceptable to you.
7	The other arm should be kept close to the belly.	Stay centred in the belly (the will), which is the source of all power.
8	Stay relaxed, but ready.	Chill, but always be ready to strike.

Alignment Of Heaven, Earth And Mankind

In modern times, there is this oft-quoted maxim that success occurs when preparation meets opportunity.

In Daoist philosophy, however, all outcomes – whether positive or negative – are a confluence of Heaven, Earth and Man.

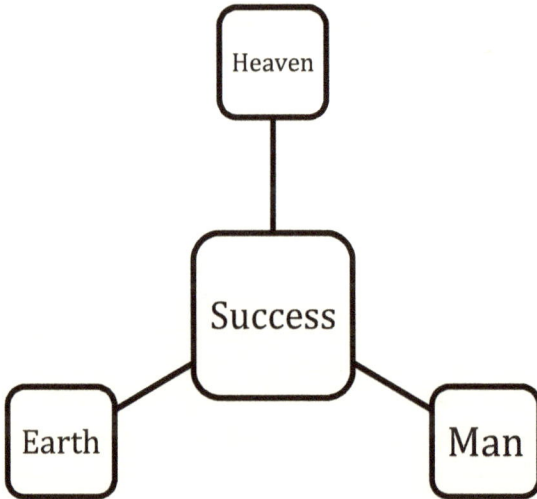

The belief is that Mankind is but one of the trinity that makes the world go round. The equation will be easier to comprehend if I gave you an example.

Suppose we could travel back in time to the early 1970s, when ABBA, David Bowie, The Carpenters and B B King were all in the rage. We know that the problem of global warming we experience today is due to the wanton neglect since the 1970s. So, we, the mankind, try to educate everyone about the dangers of CFCs, how we are destroying the ozone layer and how we should all help to lower carbon emissions. Will we succeed in preventing the situation we are facing today? Sad to say, probably not. Because although we – Mankind – are doing our best, Heaven and Earth are not aligned with us to help us succeed.

In the 1970s, the obsession was not global warming, but global cooling. A slight downward trend of temperatures from the 1940s to the early 1970s, combined with press reports that did not accurately reflect the full scope of the scientific climate literature, made the world believe that we were somehow headed for another ice age. So the tide of the times, and the general ignorance of the people then – reflecting the Heaven component – would be going against us.

The Earth component would not be helping in any way either. Economic excess, and perhaps economic overdrive, would be the rule of the day. To give an example, most products were not made to be environmentally friendly, and some of them were downright harmful. There were no biodegradable bags in those days, and factories and production plants did not hesitate to dump their waste into the rivers and oceans.

So if we did go back in time, our chances of converting the general masses to our cause would be low. We would be – metaphorically speaking – the lone voice in the wilderness, because the general tide of the times (Heaven) and the hard realities of the situation (Earth) were not on our side.

But does that stop us from trying?

No.

The sad part of the Chinese having such elaborate theories (masquerading as philosophies) is that they have been used as excuses for non-performance. Traditionally, when a Chinese fails, he will start blaming Heaven for being "not on his side". (Replace Heaven with God and you will see similarities between cultures.)

Instead of blaming Heaven and Earth, why not be like Guo Yunshen and control the Mankind factor? He was imprisoned, so definitely, Heaven was not on his side (in a lot of Hollywood movies, Guo would be said to be at the "wrong place at the wrong time"); prison was his hard reality (Earth) and he only had himself (Man) to count on.

Aligning himself, he made the best use of the situation he was in, and trained himself to be one of the most formidable fighters in Chinese history. (Of course, if he had access to a lawyer, he might have appealed. But too bad, an episode like this is hardly similar to an episode in Law & Order.)

You don't have to go through what Guo went through to understand this alignment. Just do your Santishi, not just as a martial arts practice, but in life as well.

How To Always Move Forward

The final thing I will cover in this chapter is the predominance of Xingyiquan's forward movements. Unlike other martial arts which place equal emphasis on advancing forward, retreating backwards and perhaps a couple of sidestepping and twist/turn motions, Xingyi's primary – though not only – movement is forwards. Even if there are about one or two (and I seriously mean one or two) moves that allow you to go backwards, the moves are designed in such a way where an attack is incorporated in the retreat, or in preparation for a lunge forward.

In Xingyiquan, every move is an attack and a defence.

This approach to combat is drastically different from the "The best defence is a good offence" adage that you often hear in the martial arts circles. There is also no such thing as a block then a punch; the punch is the block, and depending on your skill level, you either finish your opponent in one or two moves, or your opponent finishes you off.

It's simple, and it's straightforward.

In the same way, it is sometimes really pointless to "dance" around undesirable people in your life. An example of this would be energy vampires. We all kind of know that there are certain people in our lives who are basically detrimental to our well-being. Talking to them for ten minutes would simply take ten years away from your life. Do you still want to hang around them?

From a Xingyi perspective, I wouldn't even start this relationship. If however, you have been unfortunate in having someone close like a colleague or family member, you will have to decide if you want to continue allowing them to "suck" energy off you. If for some reason you decide to stick around, then, well and good. You made a choice which is yours and only yours to make.

If, however, you decide that enough is enough, well, then it is time to move on and move FORWARD in your own life.

Xingyi footwork, true to its nature, is linear as seen in the following illustration.

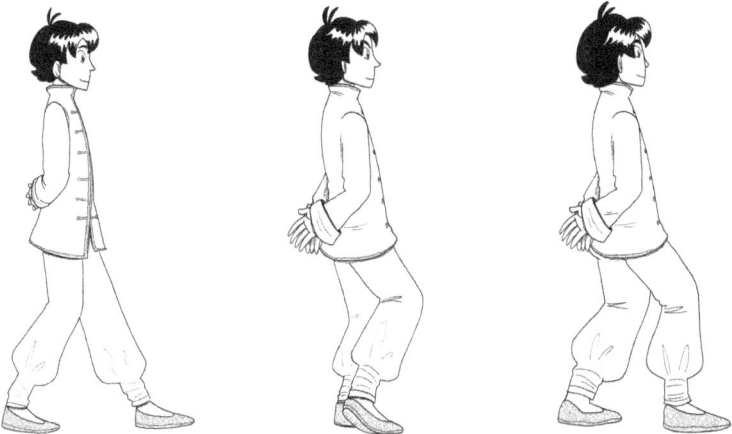

Chapter 6: Get Your Basics Right

You have seen how you should always stand upright and rooted to the ground. And you have seen how Santishi (San T'i Shih) is not just a Xingyiquan (Hsing I Ch'uan) posture but a philosophy of life. To make things better (not worse), you have seen how you should always be moving forward, always advancing no matter what happens.

But this is where the problem starts.

Whether you like it or not, the moment you start advancing, there will be those who will stand in your way. The "those" we are talking about might not be people, they might be adverse circumstances that crop up so that your advance would be a little more difficult, a little more challenging.

(It seems that the Universal Power, or God, or whoever that is out there has a way of ensuring that you are serious about your enterprise. Seriously, if there are no barriers to anything that you might want to achieve, everyone would be achieving what you want to achieve, which also means that it is not worth it. Unfortunately, the fact remains: we are all suckers for pain.)

And there is also the great social leveller to contend with. Whenever we try to be good or great, those around us will always do ALL they CAN to bring us DOWN, or in martial arts terms, to BLOCK our ADVANCE. These people might appear to be friends or family; they might be classmates or teachers; they might even be your spouse or boyfriend.

The sad thing is, there is more support for mediocrity than excellence.

Whichever the case is, you will need to have more than just the ability to stand your ground and the footwork to advance. You need the punches to help you "punch through" the obstacles you are going to face.

(No, I am not encouraging you to punch the naysayers who pour cold water over your ideas.)

The Dao? The Tao? Or The Dow (Jones Industrial Index)?

There are only five basic punches in Xingyiquan. Yup, no more, no less (and did I say that Xingyiquan is really easy to learn?). And each of these punches can be classified under one of the five elements of Daoist (Taoist) philosophy.

To help you understand the implications of such a categorisation, I will need to briefly explain how the Chinese, especially the Daoist, see the world.

To begin with, Daoism is not a religion; it is a philosophy. It is a philosophy of harmonising with nature, of living with it and tapping into the natural ebb and flow of the cosmic universe to ride out the ups and downs of life.

The essence of Daoism is captured in Daodejing (Tao Te Ching), a classic text written around 6BC by a sage called Laozi (Lao Tzu).

Like everything Chinese, the basic concept of Daoism can hardly be summarised into a single sentence. In fact, if you ask any Chinese about what the Dao – the central precept of Daoism – is, all he or she can do is to give you a vague, very imprecise explanation of what it actually is.

Without going into the details, I will do what typical Chinese do and explain what it is NOT. The Dao is NOT God, but it has all the powers of God. It is omnipotent, omnipresent and omniscient but it is not a personality. Plus, it is the origin of all creation, but it has NEVER been accorded the status of a creator.

What does it do then?

Well, as the omnipotent, omnipresent, omniscient and origin of all things alive and inanimate, it is the Source (sounds like The Matrix) and the Force (like Star Wars) of all life and power, and is extremely benevolent to everyone and everything on earth. On its own, Dao (道) the Chinese character means Way, but the word can be expanded to include meanings such as Truth, Objective or Principle.

You see the problem? I think Laozi was really out to confuse all of us when he created the concept. (But then again, maybe he was drunk and babbling away, and his students took him a tad too seriously.)

But it was Daoism that gave the Chinese the conceptual overview of life. With Daoism came the concepts of blending in with nature, synchronising with heaven and earth, and more importantly the concept of Yin and Yang.

What Is Yin And Yang?

To me, the concept of Yin and Yang is nothing more than just a basic dichotomy of life. Instead of coming up with complex rules and specifications to classify things and events, the ancient Chinese – Laozi being part of the picture as well – decided to come up with a generic guideline to help everyone make sense of everything in this universe.

The dichotomy goes like this:

Yin / Yang Illustrated	
Yin	**Yang**
Darkness	Light
Night	Day
Negative	Positive
Passive	Active
Female	Male
Down	Up
Introspection	Extroversion
Lunar	Solar
Wet	Dry
Circular	Linear
Indirect	Direct
Internal	External
Emotion	Logic
Valley	Mountain
Black	White

And the list goes on and on.

And just in case you are tempted to think of Yin and Yang as opposing forces, let me just state it clearly that they are not; instead, they should be taken as complementary forces that push, tug and pull at each other constantly, creating an equilibrium that is always changing and evolving (and that's why it is circular).

In short, Yin/Yang is about dynamic relativity in motion.

The Theory Of Five Elements

Yin/Yang is a wonderful concept. It simplifies the super-complicated world into terms that everyone can understand, and it is broad enough to encapsulate the changes that besiege the world every day.

Yet, there was a need to further classify the universe into more specific terms. Yin/Yang as a dichotomy works well at the macro level, but as a generic system, it lacks the precision that is needed to explain things at a deeper level. And that was when the Theory of Five Elements was created.

In Daoism, everything on Earth (well, they never got to the stage of space travel) can be classified under one of the five elements, which are, namely:

- Metal;
- Wood;
- Water;
- Fire; and
- Earth.

Together, the five elements engage in a constructive and destructive relationship, depending on which two elements you are pairing.

The creative relationship can be summarised as follows:

- Metal creates water;
- Water creates wood;
- Wood creates fire;
- Fire creates earth; and
- Earth creates metal.

Metal → Water
↑ Earth   Wood ↓
Earth   Wood
↖ Fire ←

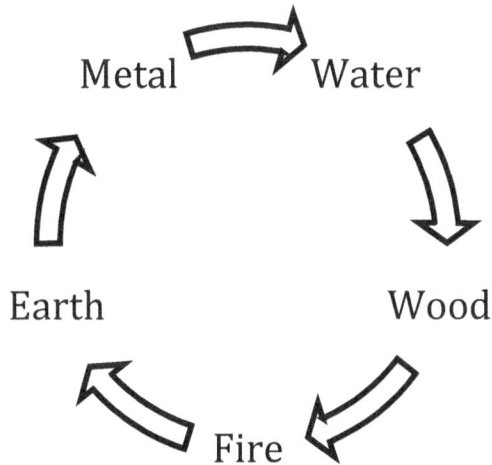

To illustrate the essence of this creative relationship, all you have to do is to take a look at what happens in the natural world.

When you heat a metal like gold, the gold melts, producing a form of molten metal, much like water (please pardon the ancient Chinese; it was the closest they could get, though you really can't drink molten metal like water. What they were really trying to explain was that when you heat metal at high temperatures, you get a form of **liquid**).

Water is absorbed by trees that give us wood. We burn the wood to get fire, and when fire burns, it produces ashes that go back to the earth (which reminds me of a college cheer that goes like this: Ashes to ashes, dust to dust, we hate to beat you but we must we must...)

And the constructive cycle continues.

And like Yin and Yang, when you have in existence a constructive relationship, you also have in existence an opposing, destructive relationship.

The destructive relationship can be summarised as follows:

- Metal destroys wood;
- Wood destroys earth;
- Earth destroys water;
- Water destroys fire; and
- Fire destroys metal.

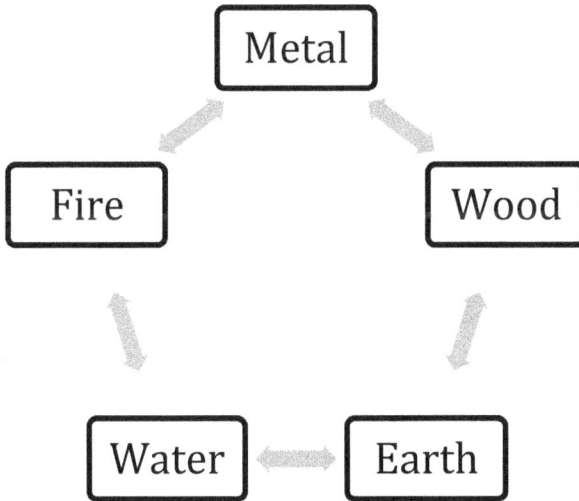

Once again, to help you understand how these pairs of relationships work, all you need to do is to take a look around you.

How does metal destroy wood? Well, don't look far; just take a look at the 1974 American slasher film, The Texas Chain Saw Massacre. In the movie, Leatherface – the antagonist – kills with a chainsaw, which is hugely metallic by nature. Other than slaughtering people, the chain saw is also useful for cutting wood and logging trees, which is how the ancients figured that metal destroys wood.

(And I think that they would have totally enjoyed watching The Texas Chain Saw Massacre. It is a more *exhilarating* way of figuring out that metal destroys wood.)

Wood "destroys" earth in the sense that the roots and stems **grip** the soil in order for trees to grow upwards. Earth "destroys" water in the sense that you can actually use sand to *cover* water, in much the same way that you will execute land reclamation. [In fact, the Chinese have a saying (they have many sayings) which goes like this: 兵来将挡,水来土掩, which sounds like "chong ching chong ching, ching ching chong ching", which means that when soldiers come to make trouble, get a general to deal with them; when flood waters come, use soil to overwhelm them.]

Water puts out fire, so that is not an issue, and fire destroys metal by melting it.

The constructive and destructive relationships that we see in the Theory of Five Elements is nothing more than a system of checks and balances to keep the world in order. Like the composition of air. Thus, while oxygen is essential for life, only about 21% of air is oxygen, while nitrogen – an inert gas – takes on about 78% of all the gases that make up air. The reason is simple: you don't want a situation where if you light a match, the whole town gets burnt down just because air is 100% oxygen. Too much of a good thing is bad.

In the same way, although the American President has been elected by the people, for the people, and is of the people, there are checks and balances in place to ensure that the President does not abuse his (Well, at the point of writing, a female president has yet to come to power. If Hillary Clinton gets nominated and wins the presidential election in 2016, I will revise this sentence) power.

That essentially, is what the five elements are all about.

The Five Elemental Punches

The five basic punches in Xingyiquan are classified according to the five elements. Each of the five punches has qualities that correspond to the attributes associated with its element.

The five elemental punches are:

- Piquan (P'i Ch'uan), or chopping punch, belonging to the Metal element;
- Bengquan (Peng Ch'uan), or crushing punch, belonging to the Wood element;
- Zuanquan (Tsuan Ch'uan), or drilling punch, belonging to the Water element;
- Paoquan (P'ao Ch'uan), or cannon punch, belonging to the Fire element; and
- Hengquan (Heng Ch'uan), or cross punch, belonging to the Earth element.

Let's go through each of the five elemental punches in greater detail.

Piquan, Chopping Punch, Metal

The first of all the five punches is Piquan. As the "leader" of the group, it is the first of all the five punches to be taught, and it is the most difficult to learn.

The difficulty in learning this punch really does not come from the complexity of the move, but the need to master the force behind it. As an internal martial art, Xingyiquan places strong emphasis on the need for 劲 (jing) (ching), which can be loosely translated to mean explosive power. However, as again, this explosive power is not the brute force you witness in boxing, but the kind of power you will feel when you release a coiled spring.

Piquan makes extensive use of this power. The fact that it is an open palm strike, rather than a fisted punch, is further proof that it is not a Muhammad Ali punch; it is actually easier to train brute force by pounding weights than to train this *jing*.

Jing takes time and effort to comprehend, before you can execute it to its desired effect. If I have made Xingyiquan sound too perfect, let me now add the clincher (this really looks and sounds like my name): if you need to enter a combat situation within the very short term, please do not bother with Piquan. It is not combat effective within a very limited time frame, because like investments, you need time to really get what this *jing* is all about.

To me, *jing* is nothing more than just muscle tension and relaxation at the right time and moment, but it is this very subtle nuance that makes it inefficient to learn. An art like boxing, karate or wrestling, however, depends *less* on this force, and is easier to train because the effects are more visible. You can measure the force of a punch, but you can't measure *jing*, like Qi (Ch'i).

Piquan isn't something you can master within one week.

That said, training in Piquan will have an almost immediate effect on your internal make-up. Because it is training in an unseen force, you will usually feel more confident – and stronger – to take on the challenges of the world. With consistent practice and commitment, your open palm strike will generate so much force that even you will be surprised at how your hands can cause so much damage to an opponent (Disclaimer: I am not encouraging you to).

Here's what the Piquan will look like. And like its name, the way it is executed resembles a person who is wielding an axe.

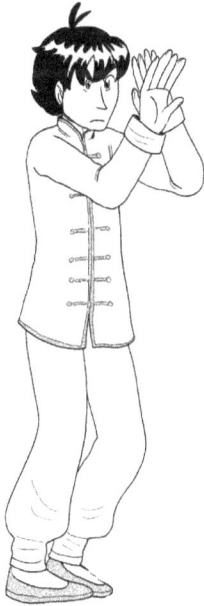

And yes, its end position looks exactly like Santishi.

Traditionally, Piquan is always practised together with Zuanquan (Drilling Punch) since the two punches naturally flow into each other. To see exactly how Piquan is practised, please search it on YouTube.

Bengquan, Crushing Punch, Wood

This is the all-time favourite of our friend, Guo Yunshen (Kuo Yun-Shen), whom I have extensively introduced to you in Chapter 4. His shenanigans with Bengquan is an all-time classic within the Chinese martial arts community, and since the release of the movie, The Grandmaster, more have come to know of his Half Lunge Crushing Punch.

Comparatively speaking, Bengquan is a lot easier to learn than Piquan. It is a lot more straightforward, and it relies less on the *jing* in Piquan.

Bengquan, or the Crushing Punch, resembles a man firing an arrow from a bow, like this:

Zuanquan, Drilling Punch, Water

Zuanquan, like its name, requires you to "drill" the punch from your belly upwards and outwards. As a printed book, it is really almost impossible for me to demonstrate the move, except to include an illustration like the following one. (Of course, you are not supposed to learn from the illustration, since it is only a comic portrayal of what you should be doing.)

As a punch belonging to the Water element, Zuanquan resembles a geyser in action.

Paoquan, Cannon Punch, Fire

Personally speaking, I think that the Paoquan is the most stylish of the five elemental punches. As the punch that belongs to the fire element, it resembles the firing of a cannon.

Cannon! Can you imagine? It was last time and some Xingyi master was able to create a punch out of a cannon!

Ok, enough of that crap. Let's have a look at how Paoquan looks like:

Hengquan, Cross Punch, Earth

The Hengquan, being a cross punch, requires you to cross your wrists before flipping them over to send one of the fists out. The power that is generated from Hengquan resembles that of a taut hand catapult. It is as if the latex band has been stretched to the maximum and released at full tension.

Once again, I would like to highlight how there are limitations to a written book. Perhaps, just perhaps, I will create an eBook with multimedia capabilities so that you can see the way all these punches are executed. But that remains to be seen so in the meantime, I would have to get you to search on YouTube to see a demonstration of this and all the previous punches.

So until then, let's have a look at what Hengquan looks like:

The Truth About The Five Elements

Together with Santishi and Xingyi's basic footwork, the five elemental punches represent the basics that you should MASTER in life before you can move on to bigger and better things. In today's fast-paced world, it is easy to forget that we need to get the fundamentals right before we can get to be phenomenal.

Want to be a great dancer? Get your basics right. Want to be an entrepreneur? Get your basics right. Want to be an awesome DJ? Get the basics right. Want to be a Xingyi master? Get the basics right.

Chapter 7: Linking Your Basics Together

Once you have got the basics right, it is time to link all the basics together. In Xingyiquan (Hsing I Ch'uan), the basics – as in the Five Elemental Punches – are linked into a form called the Five Elemental Routine. Usually mistranslated as the Five Element Linking Fist, the Five Elemental Routine combines the Five Elemental Punches into a sequence through which you can understand how they are applied, together.

The reason for the Five Elemental Routine is simple: the basics do not exist in isolation, and neither can they be utilised in isolation. In addition, the routine exists as a form of mental simulation for an actual combat situation, in which you ALWAYS win.

Some critics have argued that such sequences, or katas (especially in Japanese martial arts such as karate), are impractical since the inherent presupposition is that the practitioner doing the sequence will always emerge victorious. But these critics totally miss the point.

In rehearsing for a speech, or a ballet performance, do you rehearse for yourself to screw up? No, of course not! You mentally rehearse what you would do to get it RIGHT. You go through in your mind's eye what you would do in the IMAGINED situation.

Of course, there are multiple scenarios that can arise from a real combat situation. Many of these scenarios will not be in your favour. However, the trick is not to prepare for all scenarios – which are countless and innumerable – but to train your body to react effectively to a threat. This is most challenging since we are conditioned to the natural fight or flight syndrome, a response that is neither helpful nor effective in a potentially dangerous encounter. Preparing your body to do the right thing, however, is both helpful and effective; and to me, practising and perfecting your kata and routine is one of the best ways to condition your body to react in a predisposed manner to a perceived threat.

So rather than spending all your time trying to imagine and WORRYING what might happen to you, why not just get your basics right and spend time PERFECTING the way they are going to link together?

NB: Henceforth, where there are two illustrations per page, the illustrations should be viewed from left to right.

E.g.

Illustration 1	Illustration 2

Where there are four illustrations per page, the illustrations should be viewed from the upper left to the upper right, then lower left and lower right.

E.g.

Illustration 1	Illustration 2
Illustration 3	Illustration 4

In a case where there are two pages of illustration side by side, the illustrations should flow from the upper left to the upper right, then lower left and lower right, and to the upper left on the next page.

E.g.

1st Page		2nd Page	
Illustration 1	Illustration 2	Illustration 5	Illustration 6
Illustration 3	Illustration 4	Illustration 7	Illustration 8

The Five Elemental Routine

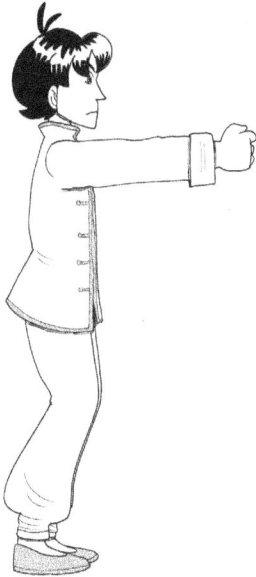

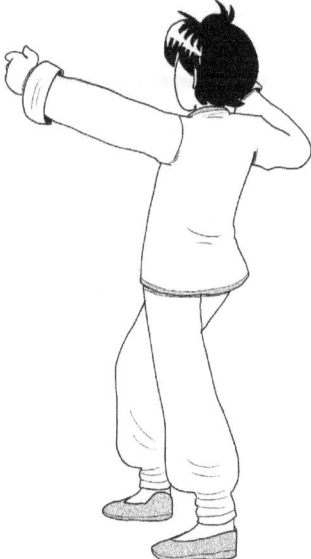

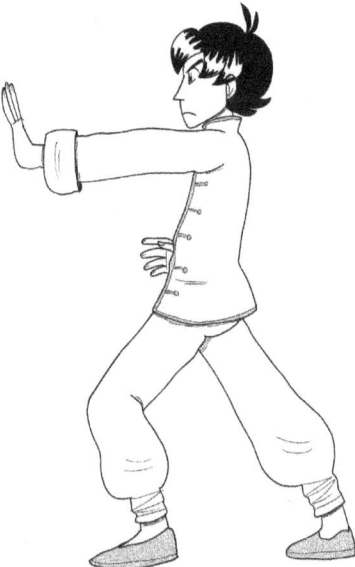

Chapter 8: Extending Your Basics

As important as they are, we can't stay stuck at the basics forever. And this is the part where I might have an axe to grind [maybe I should attempt a Piquan (P'i Ch'uan) with them] with some of these ancient (and sometimes modern-age) Chinese kung fu masters. You see, in the past, many of these ancient (and now dead) kung fu masters had a knack for making their students repeatedly do their basics for like ~ forever. The *excuse* they frequently gave to their students was that the basics are important, and that they were the foundation for all the advance moves that were to come later.

To set the record straight, I must say that I actually believe this concept. The foundation must be strong FIRST before the building is erected. But to overemphasise on the basics and to teach nothing else for years in a row is not only unacceptable today, but should also be made unacceptable in the past. The only sad thing is that the age-old reverence for elders and those in positions of knowledge and authority had lent itself to abuse in the past, and is still present in some places – especially Asia – today.

Even Guo Yunshen (Kuo Yun-Shen), someone whom I revere for his tenacity and never-say-die attitude, was guilty of such behaviour. [He made his students do Santishi (San T'i Shih) for three years in a row without teaching anything else]. And mind you, Guo Yunshen was the most systematic of the lot.

In any case, the moment you get your basics right, it is time to move on to more exciting things. In Xingyiquan (Hsing I Ch'uan), the thrill comes in the form of the Twelve Hammers and the Twelve Animals.

The Twelve Hammers' Routine

Next to the Five Elemental Routine, the Twelve Hammers' Routine is the most commonly practised kata in Xingyiquan. It is more dynamic, explosive and more physically demanding than the Five Elemental Routine, and contains advanced applications of the Five Elemental Punches.

The Twelve Hammers' Routine is thus named because the bulk of the routine makes use of the fist as a basic attacking feature. It is usually taught to students who have MASTERED the Five Elemental Punches and the Five Elemental Routine.

If you have got your basics right, learning the Twelve Hammers' Routine will propel your skill level forward. It is cool, sleek and quite a sight to behold.

And without further ado, allow me to introduce you to the Twelve Hammers' Routine.

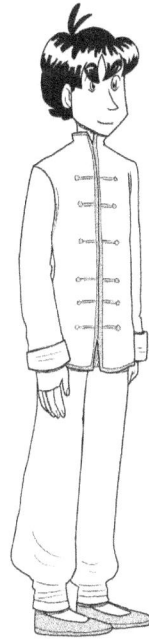

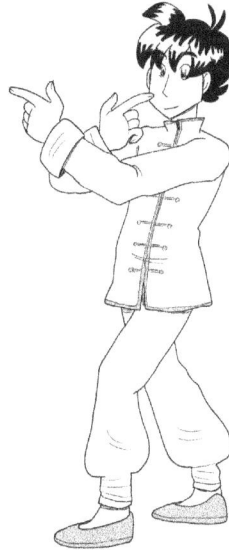

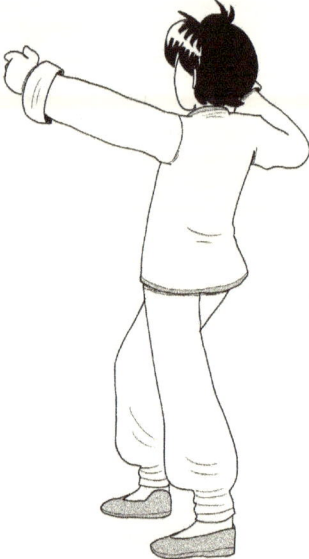

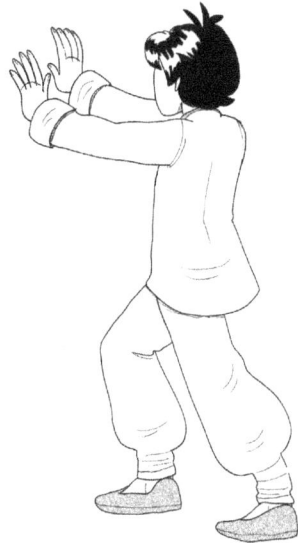

The Twelve Animals

By the time you reach this stage of your development, you are already a really advanced student of Xingyiquan. At this stage, your possibilities are boundless. As a martial art, Xingyiquan provides the opportunity for you to stretch your capabilities beyond the basics.

Not to be confused with the twelve animals of the Chinese zodiac, the practice of the twelve animals in Xingyiquan is based on the essence of the animal and not the form. As such, let's say you execute the snake attack in Xingyiquan; the shape of your palm won't look anything close to the snake form that you would witness in a bad kung fu movie.

In the same way, the look and form of your tiger pounce won't look anything like what you would witness in an old Jackie Chan movie.

Instead, in executing the snake attack, it is the relaxed tension (a paradox) of the snake that is important. If you have ever watched how cobras launch an attack – in either NatGeo or Discovery Channel, I would hate to think that you might have encountered a real cobra at close range – you will discover how they would look relaxed, and ready at the same time. The moment of lunging forward would be the exact moment where tension and relaxation are interchanged, unleashing an efficiency in speed and impact that only the most lethal of creatures can produce.

The twelve animals are as follows:

- Dragon
- Tiger
- Snake
- Monkey
- Rooster
- Swallow
- Falcon
- Sparrow Hawk

- Bear
- Horse
- Eagle
- Alligator

Due to the sheer number of animals available (yeah, there are quite a number of beasts in the world), I will only do a pictorial illustration of the first six animals in the list. (Actually, the truth is, I am running out of money for the illustrations. ☺) (And yeah, I added the alligator as a bonus! ☺)

Substance Before Style

You can obviously see by now how Xingyiquan is a martial art that places undue emphasis on substance and not style. As far as this internal kung fu is concerned, substance overrides everything; while style is just an incidental. It is a principle that has been forgotten by the masses.

Too many people today are obsessed with acting cool (and acting stupid). Seriously, if you need to act cool, you are NOT cool. The swag, style of conversation, and the poise and pose of some of the coolest people around, are borne out of a confidence in their innate abilities. If you only take on the external attributes without developing the internal ones, you are just one empty vessel.

The twelve animals of Xingyiquan is the perfect illustration of substance before style. The tiger pounce takes the spirit of the fearlessness of the tiger, without requiring the fingers to curl into the tiger claw. In the same way, when you execute the monkey move, it is the agility and nimbleness that we are looking for, and not some fanciful monkey palm that we are trying to impress the chicks with.

And as with everything in life, when substance is present, style will follow.

Chapter 9: Moving Up The Scale

The last topic that I will cover in this lengthy, and perhaps intense discussion, about Xingyiquan (Hsing I Ch'uan) and its various component parts is the topic of competence.

It was just yesterday when we all subscribed to the idea that competence was the basis and foundation of all subsequent forms of achievement. Those in the sporting arena epitomise this the best. Maria Sharapova, Tiger Woods (well, he was kind of epic in other areas as well) and Michael Jordan are all not just good at what they do, but exceptional as well. The adulation, phenomenal monetary rewards and fame were all the result of this relentless dedication to their craft.

Unfortunately, and very sadly as well, people forget this causal link between competence and reward (notice how the link isn't between effort and reward. The world does not give you any incentive for putting in effort; only your teachers will.). Instead of putting in the hard work to become outstanding, the bulk of the world has decided that looking good is more important than doing great. Where it used to be that marketing was the force to introduce a wonderful product to the world, it has become the be all and end all of all corporate efforts.

And to make things worse, misguided members of the world have begun insisting on getting the rewards BEFORE they put in the effort.

Shoots do not sprout before you plant the seeds, and if you have not sown, neither shall you reap. You can – off and on – be a freeloader and ride on the efforts of others, but the day will come – and it must come – when your incompetence and imbecility will come to the surface.

In martial arts, this is all the more true since your skill level, or the lack thereof, will become obvious as a matter of time. In the olden past, displaying your skills unnecessarily – or showing off – was an invitation for trouble. To make things worse, if your skill level wasn't on par with your display, you either end up dead or maimed.

Thus, as you progress through your study of Xingyiquan, think about how you can move from good to great. Everything else will come along as you move along.

The *show*, on the other hand, can wait.

The Four Stages Of Competence

Moving from being sucky to good is a process, and so is moving from being good to great. For those of you who are familiar with psychological theories, there are four stages of competence that you will pass as you learn the ropes to a skill, a form of knowledge or a field of specialisation.

The four stages are, namely:

- Unconscious incompetence
- Conscious incompetence
- Conscious competence
- Unconscious competence

When you are **unconsciously incompetent**, you basically don't know that you suck big time. At this stage, you are blissfully naïve about what you can do, since you think you are awesome when the reality is just the opposite. People at this stage are akin to children who know nothing about the world, having an inflated – and somewhat deluded – sense of self-esteem that has not been verified by any true experience or qualified authority in the world. And unless the individual practises an intense and rigorous form of introspection, he or she is unlikely to "wake up" from this surreal state of *happiness* which he or she takes as reality.

The most likely reason why an unconsciously incompetent individual will wake up from his deep slumber is when he is jolted into reality by an external event, usually unpleasant.

It is like seeing someone else ride a bicycle for the first time in your life, when you were a child. Without any proof or validation, you possibly thought that riding the bicycle was easy, since the rider had made it look so easy.

So with your deluded but inflated ego, you climbed on the bicycle, believing that you could replicate what you had just seen. You were unconscious about your incompetence in bike-riding, and you were taught a good lesson when the oversized bike collapsed on you.

When you get jolted from your deep slumber, you get to realise that you are not as great as you thought yourself to be. At this stage of your learning cycle, you are sorely **AWARE** of how lacking you are, in terms of skills and expertise.

You are now consciously incompetent. You are uncomfortable with the fact that there are so many things you don't know, but it is also because of this fact that you also put in a lot of effort to bridge the gap.

And that's when you put in a clear and distinctive effort to learn what you need to learn.

Since effort is the prerequisite to all competence, before long, you would be able to bridge that gap and you become **consciously competent** in your chosen field of study.

At this stage, you behave like the much wiser kid who has just learnt to ride a bicycle. You can keep your balance, you can ride straight, and you know how hard you need to pedal. But you also need to keep your eyes on the road (well, you need to do that no matter what level of competence), and you must remind yourself to keep your balance and you have to force yourself to ride straight. And yeah, both hands on the handlebars.

As they always say, practice makes perfect, and it also makes your newfound skill a permanent part of you. Given enough time and effort, you will become quite an expert at what you do. You not only can ride your bicycle with one hand on the handlebar (using the bicycle-riding analogy), you can possibly perform simple stunts without falling over. You have now become **unconsciously competent** at riding the bicycle, and it is up to you whether you want to move up the next level of learning by trying to acquire the skills necessary for complex bicycle stunts.

If you do, you go through the four stages of competence again, at a much higher level.

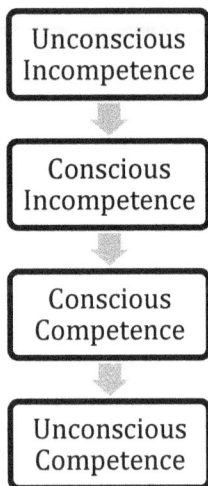

```
┌─────────────────┐
│  Unconscious    │
│  Incompetence   │
└─────────────────┘
        ↓
┌─────────────────┐
│   Conscious     │
│  Incompetence   │
└─────────────────┘
        ↓
┌─────────────────┐
│   Conscious     │
│   Competence    │
└─────────────────┘
        ↓
┌─────────────────┐
│  Unconscious    │
│   Competence    │
└─────────────────┘
```

The Four Stages Of Competence And Xingyiquan

As it should become clear to you by now, there is no end to learning, and there is no end to progress. To become real masters, whether in Xingyiquan or in life, we need this spirit of innovation, improvement and continuous learning. And it is this undying quest for the greater you that will make you the true master that you are meant to be.

When Guo Yunshen (Kuo Yun-Shen) systemised Xingyiquan learning, he also came out with guidelines to define the level of mastery a student has attained. And instead of four, he came out with three, namely, the:

- Obvious (effort);
- Subtle (effort); and the
- Leveraged (effort).

The word 'effort' has been bracketed to indicate that it is the best, yet inaccurate, translation of the Chinese character 劲 (*jing*) (ching). I first introduced this Chinese character in Chapter 6, when it meant 'force'. Like all other characters in the Chinese lexicon, the meaning of a singular character changes according to the other characters that it is used in conjunction with. Here, the character *jing* has elements of both effort and force, but I am focusing more on effort than force, because this is what I think Guo was trying to emphasise (sadly but thankfully, I have no way of confirming).

Since I have gone through great lengths to explain the four stages of competence in the previous part of the chapter, I won't go into details here since they look like duplicate systems. The only thing I would like to highlight is, unlike the four stages of competence which surfaced in the Western world in the 1970s, Guo probably introduced his concept of training and mastery in 1869, when he was about 50 years old.

And classic of all Chinese, he didn't trademark or register his concept.

I am registering his **OSL** concept on behalf of the Xingyi school, if there is such a thing.

His OSL® concept goes like this:

At the <u>O</u>bvious effort stage, you make your moves clear and unambiguous.

At the <u>S</u>ubtle effort stage, your moves are more subtle but no less powerful.

At the <u>L</u>everaged effort stage, you know of tricks and methods to generate more force with less effort.

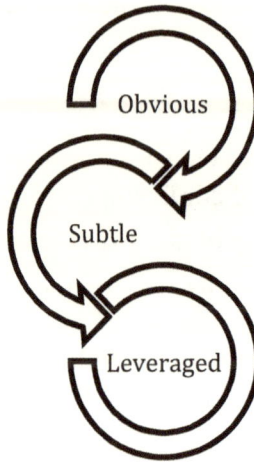

OSL® or Four Stages of Competence, it doesn't matter which frame of reference you are going to utilise. The key is to realise that becoming great is a never-ending process of learning, unlearning and relearning to put you on an upward spiral of personal achievement.

That, my friend, is the hallmark of a good Xingyi martial artist. That, my friend, is also the hallmark of a good craftsman. That, my friend, is the hallmark of anyone who has become or is becoming great and outstanding.

If mediocrity is not your cup of tea (or coffee), take a leaf from this chapter.

Chapter 10: How To Find A Good Teacher

If you have watched Kung Fu Panda (both I and II) and have taken the story too seriously, you might go away thinking that kung fu masters are either tortoises or red pandas. And if you have been a fanatic of bad kung fu movies from the 1980s, you might also be thinking that kung fu masters live on mountains.

Unfortunately – or fortunately – for both of us, neither of this is true.

And more unfortunately, you don't gain enlightenment by visiting Asia. [For some reason, books (and movies) like *Eat, Pray, Love* have a bad habit of portraying Asia as a place where something as woozy as enlightenment can be acquired in a single instant. We are no more enlightened than you are, and we also love iPhones, iPads, Xboxes and pizzas. The only thing that we have that is different from yours is our cultural heritage, which in my case is the Chinese heritage. As a heritage that is more than 5,000 years old (the Jews are the other group which can match this timeline), we are ingrained to think in a certain manner, much like how Americans and Brits are more predisposed to think in a certain manner. The advantage of a 5,000-year-old cultural backdrop is the ability to see through the passage of time, and to deduce that every idea and philosophy that is available in the world today has once been tested and tried by one of our forefathers.

The bad part of it is, sometimes, the Chinese people are a little bit tired. Having gone through tumultuous times, whether directly or vicariously, the prevailing Chinese thought patterns tend towards suspicion, distrust and pessimism. The ideas of fate, heaven's will and the limitations of mankind are all detrimental belief systems that an average Chinese has to battle and overcome in his head if he is not to fall into a state of inertia. Until about ten years ago, China had not had a good time for more than a hundred years.]

In today's world, good kung fu masters don't walk around wearing strange silky outfits [which reminds me of a friend who loved to wear silky silvery shorts. He was (and is still) kind of fat, and with his tight silky silvery shorts, it looked as though his penis (prick) and testicles (balls) (yeah, it was that disgustingly obvious) were going to burst out from within] unless there was expectancy of a major event, like a martial arts competition.

They also don't carry swords and walk around, and kung fu masters of today or the yesteryear do not fly on top of trees. These are all the stuff of Hong Kong serial drama, where Swordsman Fu Munchu not only did not have to work, he also had an unlimited supply of gold and silver which he could splurge in every inn that he went to. (And for those who are in the know about this kind of kung fu serial drama, why is it that they had to ride on horses to try to reach the capital on time, when they actually could fly to the moon in a martial arts battle? Many of my friends tell me that flying such a long distance would exhaust their internal strength, and that was why they were not taking that option, but this is simply ridiculous. If they were in a rush for time, and it was a case of life and death, and the horses couldn't make it, they should just fly there. Or are the characters in these dramas just brainless fighters?)

Instead, your average Mr Chen next door might be the martial artist who can teach you Xingyiquan (Hsing I Ch'uan), or the unassuming handyman Mr Han (sounds familiar?) who might show you the full power of a Paoquan (P'ao Ch'uan).

Which, in either case, how do you tell if Mr Chen is just a neighbour or a Xingyi (Hsing I) master? Well, there are two ways:

• You evaluate his credentials;
• You evaluate his lineage.

It's best to have both, but in a case where one precludes the other, having either one will be great.

Credentials

Ok, it's time for me to admit it, but seriously, as a martial art, Chinese kung fu sucks in its accreditation and certification processes. Unlike Japanese martial arts like karate, judo and aikido, most

Chinese martial arts schools do not practise a progressive system of grading to assess the competence of its students. This lack of accreditation extends to the instructor level as well, which makes it really difficult for both you and I to make a decision as to how good or how qualified our instructors are.

This absence of a testing process, together with the non-existence of any central governing and coordinating body for Chinese martial arts, is an offshoot of an archaic Chinese tradition of passing on the secrets to only members of the family, especially the sons. You see, if all you are concerned with is whether your son is going to master the intricacies of Xingyiquan, there is really no need for you to bother with the other students as to whether they are learning the art properly.

Which has created massive problems for the world today. Since the Chinese diaspora of the 19th century, the Chinese have been scattered around the globe, with increasing numbers settling and belonging to their lands of adoption [I am one of the classic cases. My grandfather was from China, who migrated to Singapore in the 1920s; my father was born here in the 1930s, and I am a true blue Singaporean born in this island state in 1972 (oops, you know how old I am)]. The resurgence in interest in all things Chinese also means that there is a huge demand for Chinese kung fu masters to come out into the open to teach, since for no rhyme or reason (if 9GAG is to be believed), it is suddenly cool to be Asian.

But herein lies the problem. Quacks and charlatans of all kinds have started proclaiming themselves to be masters, and going by the nonsense I watch on YouTube, this problem is not going away anytime soon.

So how do you protect yourself from these good for nothings?

The first and easiest way is to check their credentials. If they are really as good as what they make themselves out to be, they would have some form of credentials to back them up. And where Chinese martial arts are concerned, the best form of credentials would be your trophies and medals.

Like the Xingyi teacher whom I am learning from, Master Ge Chunyan (Ke Ch'un-Yan). Master Ge is a renowned pugilist from China. She was China's Baguazhang (Pa Kua Chang) champion at the national level, securing the much coveted award five times in a row (this is quite a big deal because there are MANY, MANY people in China).

In 1984, in China's National Wushu Championship, Master Ge clinched the championship title in five different categories. They are, namely, the Women's Overall Champion, Taijiquan (T'ai Chi Ch'uan) Champion, Baguazhang Champion, Long Tassel Sword Champion and Three-Person Sparring Champion.

She would later move on to become Lead Coach of the Beijing Wushu Team. Other than that, she would also get to star in quite a few movie and TV productions in both China and Hong Kong. And if you still don't know, she was fellow students with Jet Li, and was coach to actress Zhang Ziyi (Chang Tzu-I) in preparation for her role in Wong Kar-Wai's movie, The Grandmaster.

At this point in time, I see it appropriate to explain why Baguazhang is so much in the forefront of the credentials for my teacher. As mentioned in Chapter 4, after the supposed battle between Guo Yunshen (Kuo Yun-Shen) and Dong Haichuan (Tung Hai-Ch'uan), students of Xingyiquan and Baguazhang began cross-training with each other. Today, most Xingyiquan masters are experts at Baguazhang, and vice versa.

But that's where the problem lies. Instead of sharing the limelight, Baguazhang has displaced Xingyiquan in terms of fame and popularity simply because the former is more aesthetically pleasing. Xingyiquan's strength in terms of its straightforward and direct attacking behaviour simply means that it is unsuitable for the big screen.

In the same way, wushu competitions in China – and worldwide – tend to include Baguazhang as an event, and not Xingyiquan.

So if you are wondering why your potential Xingyiquan teacher has medals and trophies for Baguazhang but not Xingyiquan, don't panic. That's the nature of the *business*, and it's not something that we can do anything about for the moment. Hopefully, this book will do its job of bringing Xingyiquan into the limelight, but that's another story.

(But if your potential instructor has no medals or trophies whatsoever, but claims to be this and that, then, DO PANIC!)

So when you evaluate your potential teacher, go for the credentials.

Lineage

The other method through which you can evaluate your potential teacher is lineage.

In the previous section, I mentioned how there is an old Chinese tradition of only passing on the secrets to members of the same family, especially the sons. This, however – the ancient Chinese did realise this – caused another set of problems in the past, since capable masters might either be childless, or have children with no talent or inkling towards martial arts.

(As a side note, there were actually very capable female Chinese martial artists from the past. But they were usually taken to be of less marriageable material, since female martial artists were neither demure nor dainty, traits that have become the stereotype of Asian women. So in general, fathers tried to stop their daughters from learning martial arts, since allowing them to become fearless fighters might sabotage their attempts to settle down later on.)

Since there is no guarantee that you would be able to successfully pass on your art to the next generation within your family (In fact, even if you had a son, he might not want any of your martial arts shit since the whole world might be hounding down on him and asking stupid things like, "Your dad is such a superb fighter. Why do you fight like a sissy?" In ancient China – and perhaps to some extent today as well – people had high expectations of sons. They were supposed to carry on the family line, and if their predecessors were exceptional people, they had to carry on the tradition of excellence as well. Needless to say, many of them had daddy issues, but societal expectations and lack of treatment options meant that many of them entered their graves without resolving any of it.), they had to come up with another method to ensure continuity in their chosen field.

Which brings me to the next topic of discipleship.

In ancient China – ancient being a hundred years and beyond – discipleship was a lifelong commitment. The moment you were accepted into a sect, school or group as a disciple, you immediately promise to turn over your life to your master. Your master will – over the years – pass you his secrets, and in return, you promise to uphold his name, his clan's name, his sect's name, or his school's name until you pass on. And of course, in the course of learning his secrets, you will have to do shit for him like sweeping the floor, doing the laundry and wiping his arse (ok, that's an exaggeration).

But you get the gist.

The world has since changed, and martial arts instructors are no longer "masters". They are instructors, coaches, teachers, but they are not masters. The old Chinese name for "master" is made up of two Chinese characters, 师 (shi)(shih) and 父 (fu)(fu), with 师 (shi) meaning teacher and 父 (fu) meaning father (or parent). (And that's where the screen writers of Kung Fu Panda made a big mistake. The red panda should just be addressed as Shifu, not Master Shifu. Calling Master Shifu is calling the master Master Master.)

From the characters, you can see the relationship between the master and the disciple: the master is both your teacher and your parent; he/she will coach and guide you, not just in martial arts, but in life.

Of course, what is explained here is the *ideal* relationship. There were masters who abused this relationship, and there were disciples who were outright disrespectful, and totally disregarded what their masters taught them.

Why am I going to great lengths to explain all these?

Because there are two parallel systems running through the Chinese martial arts world.

The first one is the one we are more familiar with, which I am also under. It involves a commercial transaction, where you pay fees to learn from a martial arts instructor. In this transactional relationship, the martial arts coach makes a living by charging for teaching you what he knows. There are no obligations on both ends; the instructor doesn't really have to ensure that you do well since there are so many factors involved, and you are free to leave any time if you feel that the instructor is not good enough.

The second one is the discipleship system, which is still existent and rare. In China today, grandmasters only accept disciples whom they think are committed to the cause, and trust me, it is difficult to convince these old fogeys of your sincerity.

Incidentally, Master Ge had also trained under figures such as Feng Zhiqiang (Feng Chih-Ch'iang) and Lei Muni (Lei Mu-Ni), both legends in the field of Taijiquan. Most of all, she is the disciple of Grandmaster Sun Zhijun (Sun Chih-Chun), living (at the point of writing; I don't know how short or long this book will float around in the market) legend of Baguazhang and Xingyiquan.

To know more about Master Ge Chunyan, do visit her website at www.bafangwushu.com.

So to find out how qualified your potential teacher is, ask him or her about his/her teacher. From whom did he acquire his skill set from? Is the lineage traceable?

Which Is Better? Credentials Or Lineage?

In the ideal world, it would be best to find a teacher with both, but since the world is less than ideal, it would be good enough to find a teacher who fits one of the two criteria I have stated.

Remembering that since nobody is perfect, no teacher is perfect as well. As such, ask yourself: what are you looking for? If it helps that your teacher is a multiple award winner, you should do all you can to find one, since that teacher is more likely to make a greater impact on you.

If, however, you require a teacher to patiently coach you, then by all means: find one who will guide you slowly and painstakingly. It is always about what you want, and not what others want.

Chapter 11: Who Am I, Why I Wrote This Book And Who Should Learn Xingyiquan

The experiences that I am going to highlight are mine and mine alone and should only be used as a reference. These experiences are not to be construed in a way to mean that the reader will also undergo the same experiences, even if they have been true and verifiable for me.

As with any other aspect of life, please use logic. If you are sick, whether physically, mentally and/or emotionally, please seek the services of a qualified healthcare professional or therapist.

And before you begin any exercise, sporting activity or physical regimentation, please ensure that you are in a right state of health and fitness level by getting yourself assessed by a qualified physician.

No part of this book, whether this chapter or otherwise, should be taken as advice for your physical, mental and emotional well-being. The information presented in this chapter, and elsewhere in this book, should not be taken as substitute for the advice of a qualified healthcare professional or therapist.

At this stage, you might be wondering who this voice behind the words is. And since we have all been taught from young to never talk to strangers, allow me to introduce myself officially (though it is already kind of late in the process).

My name is Lee Lin-Cher, Lee being my family name or surname, Lin-Cher being my name. (No, I am not related to the late Bruce Lee.) My Chinese name is 李遴智 (Hanyu Pinyin: Li Linzhi; Wade-Giles: Li Lin-Chih), and for those of you who have imagined me to be a pretty babe, I apologise: I am male, and I blame my grandfather for an effeminate-sounding name.

At the point of writing this book, I am already forty-two years of age, not old enough to qualify as a senior citizen, but definitely not young enough to be classified as a youth.

I have been many things before in my life, but there are only two that matter to you at the moment.

Firstly, I was once a teacher of the English language to students from the seventh to the tenth grade, with extensive experience in the private education sector before moving on to the government education sector. The years I spent delving into the English language means that I can effectively speak the language, and write the language; and that explains why I have been able to write all this crap in the first place.

The second thing that you need to know is that I currently run a small copywriting outfit. When I mean small, I mean there's only two of us, being me and my business partner. We do copywriting for articles, magazines, books, websites and anything where you can place text on. As a copywriter providing ghostwriting services to aspiring authors and accomplished individuals, I am privy to the writing process, and more importantly, the book-publishing process.

You can find out more about my company at www.redwordtree.com. To know more about me personally, you can visit www.leelincher.net.

And the last thing that you need to know about me at the moment, is that I am NO kung fu master. Instead, I am a STUDENT of Xingyiquan (Hsing I Ch'uan), and although I have been learning it for two years, I can hardly be said to be an expert in this area. The bulk of what I understand from the art has been the result of the teaching of Master Ge, who has been instrumental in providing the foundational basis of my understanding of this wonderful Chinese skill.

Then the natural question will arise: why am I writing a book on Xingyiquan in the first place?

The answer lies in the most unlikely encounter that I would have with Xingyiquan, from about two years ago, in 2012.

My Fateful Encounter With Xingyiquan

It was July of 2012, and I wasn't in the best of health. I had just completed a gruelling month-long project with the largest real estate agency in Singapore, and the demands of what I had to do took a toll on my body.

Because for the whole month of June, I hardly slept. Work would start at nine o'clock in the morning and end at about one o'clock in the wee hours of the next morning, and this cycle lasted every day (including Saturdays and Sundays) till the project came to an end. Immediately after the job was considered done, my body decided to fall ill – I mean, very ill.

At first, it was the fever, then it was the cough. Thinking that it was just a simple case of the flu, I went to the doctor. And it was the usual case of cough mixture, paracetamol and antibiotics, which made me well for a while, until I finished my medication. And my fever and cough would return, this time with greater vengeance.

The cycle of going to the doctor for more medication, and getting well for a while until the medication ran out, would continue for two more months till I decided that something else must be done about it. It was obvious that something was not very right with my body, and mainstream medicine was finding it tough to do anything about it.

(In fact, the cough that I was experiencing was reminiscent of a pneumonia I had when I was much younger.)

And that was when I decided to approach Master Ge Chunyan (Ke Ch'un-Yan) to learn Taijiquan (T'ai Chi Ch'uan).

[Just a year prior to that recalcitrant illness (i.e. in 2011), I had found Master Ge on the internet, because I really wanted to engage in a gentle exercise like Taijiquan which could improve my well-being. Having worked hard for years, I had been plagued by this chronic fatigue which could not be cured, no matter what I took or did: supplements, vitamins, fruit, jogging, working out at the gym etc. In short, nothing worked, and I was left with not much to consider: get an internal martial art like Taijiquan and heal myself from the inside.

However, being in my head most of the time, I would think and think about a course of action till I do absolutely NOTHING about it. As an individual, I gave new meaning to the saying "paralysis through analysis".]

Fortunately for me, at that time, Master Ge didn't conduct Taijiquan classes on Fridays, which was the only day I was free. Since I had already known all about her credentials, I was adamant about only learning from her, so I told her of my situation. And that was when she suggested that I take up Xingyiquan, since it was one of the two classes she was teaching on Fridays [the other one was/is an advanced Baguazhang (Pa Kua Chang) class].

At that point in time, I didn't even know what Xingyiquan was. But since it was the only thing available to me on Friday, I took it up. And that was how I started. And I got more than what I bargained for.

Strange Effects Of Xingyiquan Training

Looking back, I found Xingyiquan training to have one of the strangest and most profound effects on my body.

The first thing was that I started feeling *weird*. My whole body was feeling very uncomfortable, and there were surges of intense thoughts and feelings that I had never experienced before. Together with the use of Traditional Chinese Medicine, my cough and fever were clearing out, but the subtle surge in "energy" or Qi (Ch'i) inside my body was getting to be quite disconcerting. In my wacko state of mind, I even suspected for a while that I was possessed by a demon or something.

And this uneasy feeling continued. But as the weeks passed, something strange happened: I was beginning to feel more energised. For the first time in all my life – and this is not an exaggeration – I actually felt that I had the **energy** and the **desire** to do things.

I started doing stuff. Cleaning out my room, planning for my future, setting goals, drafting out an action plan for myself and my company, going out to achieve; Xingyiquan had more than just physical effects. All these within a short span of a few weeks of starting Xingyiquan training.

Enough said, I was bought over.

Psychological Effects Of Xingyiquan Training

But that's not all. On a much deeper level, I was beginning to realise what was important to me in my life, and I was going to pursue it at all cost. That kind of focus, determination and will to achieve had been elusive from my life till then. All the books, tapes (yeah, I am old enough) and seminars that I had consumed had done little to propel me forward, but Xingyiquan has.

And that was when I realised that Xingyiquan was not just a martial art; it is a success philosophy and the art itself contains the engine that will drive you and me forward.

The reason for this phenomenon can be explained by one core characteristic of Xingyiquan. It quickly helps you build and store Qi in your Lower Dantian (Tan T'ien), which the Daoists (Taoists) believe to be the energy centre of the body. Traditionally, the Lower Dantian has been the vehicle of grounding in the physical world, and the more grounded you are in your belly, the more decisive, focused and clear in your actions.

The Lower Dantian is located at the point that is about three finger widths below your navel, or belly button. Just in case you think it is located on your skin, the golden stove (yup, it is also called that) is actually two finger widths behind it. (I am not too sure how you should measure this if you are ~ I mean ~ fat.)

Training in Xingyiquan is an exercise in clarity of thought and decisiveness of action. When you do Xingyiquan, you learn to translate your intentions into actions, adopting the quickest and fastest way to the goal. More importantly, your body will help you clarify your intentions, so you will have no doubt about what you need to do with your life.

That, my friend, is the treasure our ancient masters have bestowed us with.

Any Side Effects?

If Xingyiquan is so great, does it come with any side effects?

Well, other than the potential for injury in ANY sport or exercise that is NOT properly executed, I can't think of any, except one.

You might become a nasty son of a bitch, and here's why:

We have already read about how it is straightforward and direct; we have already read about how it is manifesting your intention; we also know it is linear, and goes in straight for the kill. Train long enough in this art, and your personality will manifest these traits as well.

Which means that you will take no bullshit from other people. Where in the past you might have actually been polite and more willing to give others some leeway (my way), you are now either more inclined towards calling their bluff, or not going to give them a chance to occupy a valuable piece of real estate in your mind. Which in either case doesn't make you a very nice person.

Of course, this is only my very personal experience. It might not apply to anyone else, since I am a product of my own upbringing and circumstances. (In the past, I was just too nice, and everyone took the chance to step all over me. Xingyiquan gave me the power and the temperament to be IT.)

So if you want to talk about side effects, this is the only one I can think of.

[Oh yes, like I said earlier, you might feel weird too. When your personality starts changing, you will start wondering why you are behaving in a manner that is so un-YOU. In the earlier stages of my transformation, I asked my teacher about this. She wasn't able to give me a satisfactory answer (in fact, she was quite confused, and wondered about what I was talking about).]

Who Should Learn Xingyiquan

Just like any other sport, exercise and physical regimentation, Xingyiquan is not for everyone. For an exercise to be useful, it has to be an activity that you like, and something that you wouldn't mind doing – day in and day out – for you to receive maximal benefits from the art. Not everyone is cut out for marathons, and not everyone is cut out for Xingyiquan.

Still, the CONSISTENT practice of Xingyiquan has benefits that cannot be ignored. The rewards in terms of health have already been well-documented so I shan't go into the details here. You can check it on Google, type in "health benefits of Xingyiquan" and you can get quite a few results.

There is however one group of people whom I would like to really introduce Xingyiquan to and that will be those who have been battered in the spirit.

As someone who had been plagued by inertia from the age of five till the age of about forty, I can attest to how difficult it is to get yourself up and moving when the easiest thing that we can do is to just lay low and lay disinterested. Indifference and a lack of a zeal for life are manifestations of a deeper problem, and this deeper problem usually has roots in our background and upbringing.

I don't know who you are, and what you have been through, but as someone who has survived an abusive and tumultuous upbringing, I know how tough it is to learn how to trust and believe, not just in ourselves, but in the inherent goodness of life and the worth of any cause in the world. For close to fifteen years, I psychologically shut myself from the world, denying myself of my worth and what I deserve. It was almost as if I never existed, whether we are talking about physical, mental or emotional existence.

For most of my life, I behaved as if I NEVER existed.

And this lack of self-worth manifested in every area of my life: my personal and professional relationships, my career, my business, my achievements...

Xingyiquan changed all that. I know it sounds slightly ridiculous, but this art itself has been one of the two reasons how my view and attitude towards life took a roundabout turn (I will tell you what the other one is in the next chapter).

And that is why I have written this book. Despite all its goodness, this kung fu form has barely received the kind of attention that it should receive. Without the limelight, individuals like you and I can hardly have access to all its benefits, the gift of rebirth and positive transformation that is available to all of us, as long as we are willing to commit ourselves to the path.

It is time we stand up for ourselves, and to stand firm on the ground with our heads held high. It is time for us to embrace the Xingyi spirit.

Chapter 12: Healing Yourself From Deep Within

No book on personal achievement would ever be complete if the topic of healing ourselves from deep within is left out. And in this chapter, I am going to introduce you to a healing modality that can be a potent combination with Xingyiquan (Hsing I Ch'uan). But before that, allow me to relate how I found this healing modality.

Due to the less-than-ideal childhood and teenage years that I have had, I have always had an issue with personal achievement. In the previous chapter, I mentioned how I behaved as if I didn't exist, and this lack of self-worth manifested itself in many ways, the most notable being my lack of career achievement.

Without mincing my words – and allowing myself the harshest of all criticisms – I had been nothing but a loser until I found Xingyiquan. In Asia, especially in Chinese societies, how much money you have in your bank accounts, the kind of houses that you stay in, and the job that you hold, are lenses through which society is going to see you whether it is through your own effort or not. This societal backdrop that I live in, together with my traumatic growing up years, was going to be a formula for disaster for me.

Having no advantage of a silver spoon in my mouth, career advancement was the only social mobility tool I had in my disposal, a tool which I wielded with dismal capacity.

For the bulk of my life since I stepped out to work at twenty-four years of age, I had experienced much difficulty in properly holding down a job. My desire to achieve was there, but I was unable to properly relate to my bosses and co-workers, and the way I thought was too wayward for most people to handle. In short, I was sort of a renegade. But the renegade behaviour was not commensurate with enough confidence to violate the norms of society, not to mention trash it.

In short, I didn't have the "balls" to get what I wanted, and to ignore everyone else.

So if you were to take a look at my career history, you would see multiple starts and stops, a sign of a misfit who couldn't figure his way out in the place he was in.

[It was only much later on (and I really mean much later on, like last year, in 2013) that I realised that I was suffering from the effects of post-traumatic stress disorder (PTSD). What I was going through was nothing more than what war veterans go through.]

Due to the mismatch between what I wanted to achieve and what I was actually achieving, I had always been a seeker, on a lookout for all sorts of "cures" that would help with my cause, "cures" such as:

- Motivational books (yup, I had shelves of them);
- Motivational tapes and CDs (I listened to anyone who could promise me something);
- Motivational seminars (I paid thousands for them for a five-month high);
- Goal-setting, planning and organisational tools;
- All sorts of New Age religious movements;
- Churches preaching the prosperity gospel;
- Meditation classes promising to "unleash" the innate power that you have;
- Subliminal tapes and CDs (oh, these were expensive);
- Affirmations (yes, I wrote them in the present tense and recited to myself religiously);
- Visualisation exercises (I saw what I wanted in my mind's eye, but they never came);
- Feng Shui (yup, I have fish tanks and fountains as well);
- Irish clovers (they did bring luck, to the guy who sold me the thing);
- Vision boards (I really cut out pictures of all I wanted from magazines and all that);
- Jade (I bought a US$1500 piece of nicely-crafted jade from Taiwan; the owner got richer);

- Psychotherapy (where the psychologist gets me to talk and talk); and
- Past life regression (I was a ninja in my past life ☺).

You can see what a fool I had been, but I really didn't know better.

And really, it's not as if the tools didn't work. All of them are potent in their own right, but until you find the **REAL REASON** of what's holding you back, every one of these tools will really have a limited impact on you.

So, one thousand and one tools later, I was still where I started, except that I was more broke than ever, and older than before. That was when my lucky break came.

Going Far Back For The Root Causes

Like it or not, the persistent problems that hound us for the bulk of our lives usually have their root causes from far back, and I mean way far back, like in our past lives. For those of you who are more aware, you probably know that this is not our first time here.

Just like religion and politics, the subject of past lives can become an emotionally-charged topic. As far as conventional science is concerned, there is no proof of past lives, and future lives. If this chapter is going to bother you, or you do feel that this topic is against your personal convictions whatsoever, please skip this totally.

Whether past lives exist is not the topic of discussion here. If you need proof of its existence or otherwise, please feel free to do your own research and reading. A lot of stuff has been written on this topic, and if it feels significant enough for you, you should do the right thing by proving or disproving it to yourself.

But back to my lucky break. It was in 2009, and I was the editor of a complementary therapy magazine when I was told to do a feature article about this healing modality called Spiritual Response Therapy (SRT). Doing research over the internet prior to an interview with a local practitioner, I would soon conclude that this was nothing more than just a con job, with me expressing my reservations to my publisher about how I didn't believe that such spiritual hocus-pocus could even have any effect on the client.

In short, I was wrong about my initial assessment.

My meeting with the practitioner didn't get off on a very good start. Within minutes of meeting him, I deduced that he was a nut case, and my comfort level with him was less than ideal. In any case, the man volunteered to "clear" me, which I promptly declined but the man never got to understand. He "cleared" me against my will (how he did that, I don't know).

The next day, I woke up, feeling off and *weird*. (Why is it that everything involving healing always makes someone feel *weird*?) I felt a lot lighter, as if something had been lifted off my shoulders. And what used to set me off the wrong way no longer had power over me. All these benefits I experienced without the practitioner clearing me in my presence, and without me having to believe a single bit of it.

Intrigued by what this was all about, I went on a rampage, reading up on anything and everything I could find about SRT on the internet. What I was most concerned about was whether it was "black magic", and whether any "evil force" had taken over me. The good news is, after five years of intensive clearing, I can say good things about this wonderful gift that has originated from the United States of America. It has been the reason for all the good things that happened after 2009 (including me "stumbling" upon Xingyiquan), and it has been one of the two critical triggers for my growth and understanding.

And no, there is no evil force, and there is no black magic.

Healing yourself from deep within will give you huge payoffs in terms of what you are trying to achieve in this world. As a healing modality, SRT works on the same principle as Xingyiquan: as an internal martial art, Xingyiquan unblocks Qi (Ch'i) flow through the body by utilising direct and unambiguous moves, while SRT helps us release discordant energies at the soul level by accessing knowledge of unseen root causes that plague us in our everyday lives.

And like Yin and Yang, SRT works on the spiritual planes, while Xingyiquan works on the physical planes. The two work hand in glove, if you are willing to give yourself a chance. Like the way I had it; from 2009 to about 2012, I was working on myself from deep inside, but from 2012 onwards, it was manifesting what I want on the outside.

To know more about SRT, you can visit www.spiritualresponse.com or www.spiritualresponsetherapy.org.uk.

How Do I Get Started In My Healing Process?

Well, before you get started in anything, let me first give you the irritating disclaimer (I have to do this because there have been instances where people really misconstrue what I say):

The experiences that I have highlighted earlier are mine and mine alone and should only be used as a reference. These experiences are not to be construed in a way to mean that the reader will also undergo the same experiences, even if they have been true and verifiable for me.

As with any other aspect of life, please use logic. If you are sick, whether physically, mentally and/or emotionally, please seek the services of a qualified healthcare professional or therapist.

No part of this book, whether this chapter or otherwise, should be taken as advice for your physical, mental and emotional well-being. The information presented in this chapter, and elsewhere in this book, should not be taken as substitute for the advice of a qualified healthcare professional or therapist.

The first step is to accumulate knowledge. You need to know what SRT is and be REALISTIC about what it can do for you. Like any other healing modality, SRT is no magic wand, and undergoing it requires commitment on your end to not only cooperate, but to make adjustments in your life where necessary. And if you haven't realised it, it is ONE of the many modalities out there that can change your life for the better (which one you choose is a matter of preference).

So visit the websites first and see if it is for you.

The next thing, of course, is to look for a practitioner who can help you. On the Spiritual Response Association (SRA) website (www.spiritualresponse.com) is a list of certified consultants under the "Consulting" tab. Click on it and scroll through the list. If anyone catches your eye, make contact with the consultant and ask him/her what he/she can do for you.

While it has never been said, each practitioner has his/her own strengths and fields of expertise, and the kind of results you can get is dependent on the match between what you want to achieve and what they are excellent at doing.

So please do your homework. Choosing an SRT practitioner is no less significant than choosing a doctor who can help you with your ailments. If you really want to heal from your trauma, you will have to practise due diligence.

And this is the part where I introduce my SRT consultant to you, Eric Scott.

Since 2009, I have personally known a few SRT practitioners with various strengths and foci, but Eric is one of those few interesting personalities that I will bother to write a testimonial for. As an individual, he doesn't talk, or write much, since our only correspondence is through email. However, a clearing session with Eric possibly yields more results than you can ever expect, and definitely he is very Xingyi in style (although I don't really think he knows Xingyiquan); not saying much, but going straight to the source of your problem.

So if you want no bullshit in your clearing, Eric is my recommendation.

You can visit Eric at srtnow.com. He has a few interesting videos there, so you might want to take a look.

Working With A Higher Spiritual Force

Remember how I mentioned in one of the previous chapters that success is a confluence of three factors, of Heaven, Earth and Mankind? Because as much as we want to believe that Mankind is all strong and powerful, we need to acknowledge that life is inherently frail.

We need as much support and backup as we can find, and to me, nothing is more comforting than to realise that we are not alone in our pursuit of personal achievement. And that's where the topic of guardian angels, spiritual guides, deities and gods kicks in.

As a Chinese Singaporean, most people would expect me to be either Daoist (Taoist), Buddhist or possibly Christian in my spiritual orientation.

Unfortunately for the many people who guessed it wrong, but fortunately for me who got it right (for myself), I am neither of the above.

Instead, I am a deep believer in Lord Ganesha, the elephant god-deity from the Hindu tradition. As the remover of obstacles, god of success, knowledge and writing, Lord Ganesha goes over and beyond the role of just being a super-being that is to be revered and worshipped.

His entire image and outlook hold deep symbolism for both you and me, and through the study and understanding of such symbolism, we will be able to understand the true elements that determine if we become one of phenomenal greatness, or one of unprecedented disaster.

A lot of material about Lord Ganesh has been posted on the internet.

As the author of this book, I ask of you to research on the web what this great Lord can teach you about greatness, success and personal achievement. You will love what he represents, and you will definitely learn a thing or two about what being outstanding is all about.

To know a thing or two about Lord Ganesha, you can visit http://sttemple.com. Under the "Sri Layan Sithi Vinayagar Temple" tab, click on "Worship of Vinayagar" option. There, you will know of the significance of the worship of Lord Ganesha (also known as Lord Vinayagar), and the story of how he got his elephant head.

For those of you who are in Singapore or who might be visiting Singapore, a trip to the Sri Layan Sithi Vinayagar Temple (at 73, Keong Saik Road, Singapore 089167) will be one of the most fruitful journeys that you can ever undertake in your lifetime. It's the temple I visit on a regular basis, and it's the one place that has provided me solace and comfort in times of distress and pain.

As again, never take my word for it. See it and experience it for yourself.

Going Beyond Yourself At All Levels

Finally, we have reached the very end of this book. As cliché as it sounds, personal achievement is a journey, not a destination. Just like all roads lead to Rome, there are many paths that you can take to success and greatness.

To me, Xingyiquan is the best road that I can take, and I hope that it is also the road for you. Remember: there is no need to suffer unnecessary pain, and where pain is necessary, always use it as the foundation to the next level of greatness.

With that, I am going to end this quest that I have set out to do, to put all I know about this wonderful art on the table so that more people will know about it, and more people will embrace it.

Earlier on in the book, I mentioned once or twice about the Xingyi spirit. Some of you might be wondering what this "Xingyi spirit" is all about.

To that, I will point you to the lyrics of "We Own It" by 2 Chainz and Wiz Khalifa for the 2013 action film "Fast and Furious 6".

I never fear death or dying

I only fear never trying

I am whatever I am

Only God can judge me now

One shot, everything rides on

Tonight, even if I've got

Three strikes, I'mma go for it

This moment, we own it

Yes, my friend, that is the Xingyi spirit. Never fear, always try, and put everything you have got into every shot that you take. That to me, is already success. And in Xingyi, we always say that all it takes to kill a raging bull is one year of Xingyi training (well, please note, it is only a metaphor).

You don't want to kill a bull; that's animal cruelty. But you will promise me that you will punch through every obstacle that stands in your way to a worthy cause.

With that, I wish you all the best, in everything that you do.